a

b

Wrestling In Deep Waters

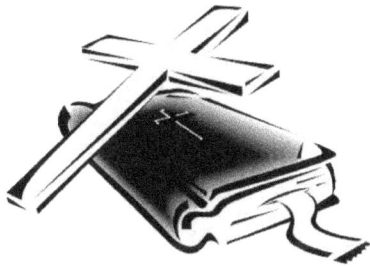

The Paradox of Evangelism's Growth

WRESTLING IN DEEP WATERS

The Paradox of Evangelism's Growth

Editor & Designer

Sherman A. Jones

Cbookspublishing and Bookstore
Cbookspublishing.com

WRESTLING IN DEEP WATERS
The Paradox of Evangelism's Growth

Cbookspublishing and Bookstore

619 Copeland Dr.

Cedar Hill, Texas 75104

www.cbookspublishing.com

ISBN: 978-0-9849733-4-7 (Hard-copy)

ISBN: 978-0-9849733-3-0 (Soft-copy)

Published by Cbookspublishing

A Division of Cbookspublishing and Bookstore
619 Copeland Dr. Cedar Hill, Texas 75104

An American Publishing Company

WRESTLING IN DEEP WATERS

The Paradox of Evangelism's Growth

"Initial Remarks"

"We do not wrestle

Against flesh and blood, but against

principalities, against powers,

against the rulers of the darkness of

this age, against spiritual hosts

of wickedness in the

heavenly places"

 (KJV Eph. 6:12).

Let both grow together until the harvest: and at the time of harvest I will say to the reapers, Gather ye together first the tares, and bind them in bundles to burn them: but gather the wheat into my barn. (KJV_Mt 13:30)

"The words of a man's mouth are as deep waters, and the wellspring of wisdom as a flowing brook" (KJV Pr. 18:4).

This Book was printed in the Unites States of America

CONTENTS

Published by Cbookspublishing

Memo

To: All
From: The Author
RE: God's Revelation in All Things

Dear Reading Critic:

This prelude, *to our "preface" on the next page*, extends the following:

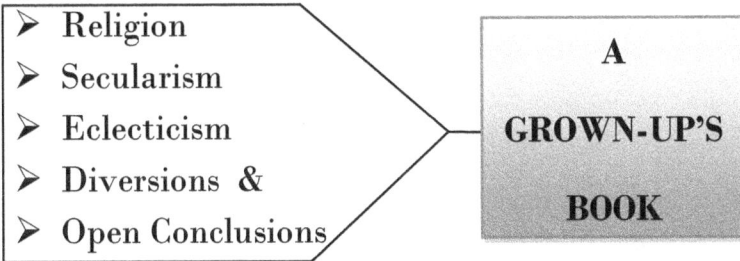

➢ Religion	**A**
➢ Secularism	
➢ Eclecticism	**GROWN-UP'S**
➢ Diversions &	
➢ Open Conclusions	**BOOK**

Sidebar >>>>> The rock and roll singing group, "The Temptations," sang a song by the name of "*Ball of Confusion*," which receives this sidebar's prelude to our preface seeks relevancy, whereas, you get to be the "judge." However, you must stop your reading [for a moment] and go to your computer and type in this URL <http://www.youtube.com/watch?v=miZWYmxr8XE>. You must listen to the song to make your decision. Pay close attention to a new used word in the song "**Great-Googa-Mooga-Booga!**" We need a ruling from you— "the reading judge"—as to its admissibility. This means give us **"review"** after read this book.

*

**

PREFACE

"The fool has said in his heart, there is no God"—David (Ps.14:1).

In this book, *Wrestling In Deep Waters*, tares and wheat are mixed wordings of gospel and gossip (man's "b—s"), which affect spirituality in worship. This contrast causes a great wrestle in the waters of the righteous, and the unrighteous wanting to see God. This book is of no familiar formula! However, this book is a book for general information, spiritual enlightenment, and reading enjoyment. Lest we forget, God is our "refuge in the day of affliction" (KJV, Jer. 16:19. The author of this book is not God! This author has no heaven neither a hell that he can magically wand you to as a reward or as a punishment. *Wrestling In Deep Waters* is just a good book for us to read in the enjoying or hating thereof. You Choose! The narrative formula offered throughout this book will be in the spiritual researching the King James bible, other religious sources and sources. We acknowledge that the King James' version of the bible is not the only version. This author has a degree in theology as a preacher and teacher and have studied secularly. As to researching, if, you want to know all, the first bible was of Latin origin around 380

AD. We further understand and know that the first
mass produced bible was the Gutenberg Bible by
Johannes Gutenberg from the city of Mainz, Germany,
between 1452 - 1455.[1] Now, that we have gotten that
out of the way, it is here with understanding—the
coming enjoyments in this book are of many facets,
fascinations, and familiarities. As to retaining you,
the scholarly minded, the inner workings are the catch-
up extrapolations of divine Biblical inspirations
accenting all knowledge, *Wrestling In Deep Waters*. Yes!
These also includes biblical scriptures! Let it be heard
the more:

> God is our refuge and strength, a very present
> help in trouble. Therefore, will not we fear,
> though the earth be removed, and though the
> mountains be carried into the midst of the sea;
> Though the waters thereof roar and be troubled,
> though the mountains shake with the swelling
> thereof, Selah. There is a river, the streams
> whereof shall make glad the city of God... (KJV
> Psalms 46:1-4).

---

[1] Ideafinder. "Did you ever wonder what was the first mass produced book?"
The Great Idea Finder . 1997 - 2007 .
http://www.ideafinder.com/features/everwonder/won-printbook.htm
(accessed April 10, 2013).

"While our country has made great strides in breaking down the barriers which for so long denied equal opportunity to all Americans, we are not yet the beautiful symphony of brotherhood of Dr. King's dream." — Adam Schiff.

Published in the U.S.A., *Wrestling In Deep Waters* see this country with impressive strides in the breaking down of the color barriers that for so long denied equal opportunity to all Americans. However we are not yet that beautiful symphony of brotherhood spoken about in Dr. King's "The Dream Speech. — Adam Schiff.

Going forward, *Wrestling in Deep Waters* as a religious book juxtaposes me sitting and listening to one of the greatest symphony to be published. It is the music in the background of Beethoven *Ninth Symphony* steering the peaks and valleys of this book as I now write for you. In the continue reading, we will allow ourselves to ride the peaks and valleys of the inclusions to a finality. This is what makes a good "anything." This movement from inception to a closing stage allows God to fill the gaps as a "bridge" over a river or trouble waters. And for some of you **eaters**, this is like a good steak accented with a good gravy, marinadeed, and slowly cooked for satisfying the spirit of our soul. Come with me and my symphony, as the drums beat with a thundering drum roll! This is no lackluster in speech nor printed page that disregards us as the spiritual, mature audience. Continuing to write this book, it is as to the mastery of Beethoven's Symphony No. 9. *Wrestling In Deep Waters* punctuates the great exclamation that is found in joy, which probes and prods us in our many living concertos that crescendos as did Beethoven's Symphony No. 9, in his listeners' ears. As Beethoven his listerners, *Wrestling In Deep Waters* has you.

"I have found the paradox that if you love until it hurts, there can be no more hurt, only more love." — Mother Teresa

The depth of every book is its narrative; the same as with a lover serenading him/her to be loved at the mating call of the wild. Caution: Beware of the wolves! Many "a hunter" has been caught by the game. In God there is no game, and, if so, God would be a game of love for/in us. This is a **love/hate story** for us to share.

With *Wrestling In Deep Waters* keeping us, I am reminded of a mother who took her daughter to a hospital. Her daughter was near dead from an over dose of drugs. The hospital and doctors did all that "**they**" knew to save her. Finally, one of the doctor came from the child's room turning to the child's mother stated, "I do not know what else we can do to save her." The hospital and these doctors has lost hope. In their minds, this little girl would not survive. To the surprise of the doctor, the mother said, "Everything is going to be alright." The doctor rejoined and asked, "What do you mean?" The girl's mother said, "I've prayed for my child. She is in the hand of God, and the Lord will save her." While the mother was yet speaking, the little girl, which the doctor thought had no hope, she opened her eyes and said, "Mama!" To the astonishment of the doctors, the mother looked at the little girl and then toward the doctors and just smiled. The doctors hurried away scratching their heads. It is in the book—*Wrestling in Deep Waters*—all is in God's hand.

"Any fool can turn a blind eye but who knows what the ostrich sees in the sand." – Samuel Beckett

Much of this book, *Wrestling In Deep Waters*, the enemy (Satan) sows or plant tares(his word) among the wheat(God's word) is the *paradox of evangelism's growth*. Sorting this out will cause many to scratch their heads wanting to give up, but you cannot. As to the forewarning, Wrestling in Deep waters is an unusual book. Is there such a thing as being uncommon? Would it be in forewarned? Some books are as this book with transcendences as to all learned disciplines. Is this uncomon coming from a nobody to you? Most of our troubles in life are brought about under a certain belief with a lack of prayer—"heads stuck in the sand of mental chaos." This book is about positioning and choosing the best of all disciplines under/within the context of "who God is" not to persuade you as to anything nor who God should be in experience of receiving his love. However, this book will in the wanting to endeaver do much fruit inspecting along the way. This will be a once in a lifetime opportunity that we receive high-quality pleasure "holding on" to the good in the supremacy of God's power as we humbly reverence his might. So, here we just holding on, holding on, and holding on—not wanting to let go as time points in water to another side. Well! This is the right book for our satisfaction as we continue the "*Wrestling In Deep Waters!*"

He it is, who coming after me is preferred before me, whose shoe's latchet I am not worthy to unloose" (KJV Jn 1:27).

In these swelling deep waters, our wrestles are these collected intellects--as the best of the best being the preferred or the not-so-preferred; whereas, the "better" (God) cannot be bested by anything or anyone! In this book, *Wrestling In Deep Waters*, the author [Sherman A. Jones] has chosen "variety" as a supplying style with an attempt not violating the scriptures! Nonetheless, it is here now as we once more look at the other side of the coin that we know that all will never agree any one thing, and there will always be argumentations. At to each point in argumentation and for argument's sake, it will be several models styles used in/within the rhetorical importations. With a preacher, prophet's prerogative, the privilege will be leisurely used. More than most, *Wrestling In Deep Waters* will adopt the Classical or Rogerian argumenation's model of persuation in this book to authenticate and substantiate clarifying points that might not resonate in the general knowledge of the reader. Although, the author of this book has graduated from the school of law. This author will not be using much of the Toulmin model of argumentations, which are used in field of law as did the Biblical Pharisees that taunted Jesus with school boy's "mockings." Beware, all of you sanctimonious, holier-than-thou, die hearts. Just enjoy the book!

"I am fundamentally an optimist. Whether that comes from nature or nurture, I cannot say. Part of being an optimistic is keeping one's head pointed toward the sun, one's feet moving forward. There were many dark moments when my faith in humanity was sorely tested, but I would not and I could not give myself up to despair; that way lies defeat and death. "—Nelson Mandela

This book is just a plate's counter or a table where the full meal gets a display. These waters on the buffet's table are God's word mixed with Man's word .

However, it is your choice as a reader in/with selectivity of sanctifying your beliefs as to further nourishment. At the dinner table, there is plenty food for all relating to thought processes. The hungry that eats shall live. Jesus said, "For their sakes, I sanctify myself that they also might be sanctified through the truth" (KJV John 17:19). This leans more to truth "that they might sanctify and cleanse it with the washing of water by the word" (KJV Eph 5:26). Even, babe must eat; however, meat is not good for their digestive system. On the table, you decide what you will eat or will not eat.

Wrestling In Deep Waters is the swelling in the belly. This is all about our appetite and diet—spiritual food or not—the table has a mixture of food. How are you dieting? On the table there are tares and wheat. However, and still, the hungry mayand must eat! This book, *Wrestling In Deep Waters*, wants you to eat and be filled with joy. Before the cooking or preparing of the table, there is this mad rush to the grocery store. The decision is this: What to get "Greens" or "Meats?" The author—as to the raised question—acknowledges there is a bit of irony here, but this is just a matter of taste or a the needed for exercise. This is in the diversified but not as a lie [Tares = lies]. This book is not the disputing or embracing of any given philosophy within religion or secularism, neither will there be "an adding or taking away from the prophecy of the book [bible]" (KJV Rev 22: 18-19).

"The first time someone shows you who they are, believe them."—Maya Angelou

In this book, *Wrestling In Deep Waters*, there will be many thought provoking insertions. Many of these will make the real you show up in these faith waters. We are of the opinion that is not so important as to who other think that your; but rather, you know who and whose your are in the context fo serving.

In this book, citation of scriptures and references' will be of a combo "APA" format or an inserted footnote using the "Chicago" format. The adornments as points of view will receive no endorsement by the author of this book, *Wrestling In Deep Waters*. Nevertheless, the author of this book, *Wrestling In Deep Waters*, will not give way to limitations or restraints.

"God sends no one away empty; except, those who are full of themselves."— Dwight L. Moody

Wrestling In Deep Waters denotes the spiritual in all life connoting the many similarity of "tares and wheat" in the "Paradox of Evangelism's Growth" pilgrimage associated with the "Holiness of God." Let us not forget that a paradox [absurdity] is man's word and will pretend to be "God's Holy Word." This book, *Wrestling In Deep Waters*, points to the author's distinct talents in the writing world of communication. The first publication by this author was a military memoir associated with the Vietnam episode, and the book is titled, *Teardrops of War*. "*Teardrops of War*," was published in the rough (no professional editing) and have sold the most copy with its unique quality. Poetry and Beyond is the author's second book, a book of poems and essays mixed with philosophical thoughts. This third book, *Wrestling In Deep Waters* [Tares and Wheat—"The Paradox ofEvangelism's Growth"], is bejeweled and is steeped in prophecy taken from the book of Ezekiel receives all of biblical living in life's past, present, and future as we study and refer to the dispensational times of God.

"*It is easier for a camel to pass through the eye of a needle than for a rich man to enter the Kingdom of Heaven.*"— Jesus (Luke 18:25)

Wrestling In Deep Waters, as a book, the arguments are within the scope of humanity's growth. Growth— in the context relationship with God—might seem insane or contradictory; nevertheless, the rhetoric can or may be true. However, the truth is still the truth, which captures and creates knowledge. When there is agreement, God's word gives moral intrinsic value. The irony and the analogy are to the looking at the cake, which remains the same no matter how many times you change the frosting. In this book, we allow ourselves to see the voice of man in the usage of God's word. It his here where man uses exaggerations to the swelling of the jaws as hyperboles throughout history have made many platforms. Over time these have become devalued, diluted "unrighteousness" in "the becoming wiser and weaker" with self-righteousness as the paradox in the growth of man's progression.

"The water and the word are not always metaphorically synonymous. The separation can be as to a physical juxtaposed to the spiritual. This will always leave a person [for the most part] more watery than the word— drowning in himself."—Sherman A. Jones.

This book, *Wrestling In Deep Waters*, looks at Christianity and religions of many kinds with man reasoning within evangelism with God abhorring bigotry and intolerance. The "tares and wheat must grow together" (KJV Matt. 13:30). Even, the self proclaimed advantage—the self proclaimed owners of the marketplace's goods and conversations, which flow— is safe [so to speak] for now. "Living life is not just the happening in churches or from one book relating to religion!" Religion can be the church, one's politics, fraternity affiliations, clubs, hate-groups, and—even, time relative to every evaluation. In this book, we will learn how "Tares and Wheat" combine to create the swelling and the smelling. For the saved, God's word is unadulterated faith, which exposes bigotry, hatred, and evil imaginations of all enemies.

"Nevertheless, it seems reasonable to say that the postmodern's initial concern is to de-naturalize some of the dominant features of our way of life; to point out that those entities that we unthinkingly experience as "natural" (they might even include capitalism, patriarchy, liberal humanism) are, in fact, "cultural"; made by us, not given to us."—Linda Hutcheon

As to an end, the end will be with God as it was from the beginning. A victorious finish over sin will be at the separation where tares will be burned and the wheat will be eaten. Aside from the seemingly negatives (religion, capitalism, patriarchy, liberal humanism, or conservatism), the end is always positive if we are are faithful under God. Solomon says to us, "Let us hear the conclusion of the whole matter: 'Fear

God, and keep his commandments: for this is the whole duty of man. For, God shall bring every work into judgment, with every secret thing, whether it is good, or whether it be evil'" (KJV Eccl. 12:13-14). *Wrestling In Deep Waters* [Tares and Wheat, The Evangelistic Growth's Paradox!]

The last word— before the beginning, belongs to Jesus, *"Let both grow together until the harvest: and at the time of harvest I will say to the reapers, Gather ye together first the tares, and bind them in bundles to burn them: but gather the wheat into my barn"* (KJV Matthew 13:30). — Jesus

Acknowledgements

I want to extend my profound pleasure to the countless pastors and educators who contributed significantly to developing my several abilities in the framework of preaching, teaching, researching, and writing. My greatest expressed appreciation goes to my God, who is the head of the church, and the creator of all life who has endowed me with, at least, an average intellectual capacity.

Many thanks also to the many professors who demanded I write scholastically modulating my talents. As a graduate of Kaplan University, I am grateful for my law professors and for the education that I received from the School of Criminal Justice and Legal Studies.

It is with further appreciation—as a student of the gospel and the law that advanced my writings in theology as I have used research methodologies learned to support my credibility. It is also and in addition my knowledge of business principles, and general accounting, which allows me now to publish from my own publishing company today. There are many deserving of accolades, which have helped me get to this point of satisfaction, which brevity will not permit me to acknowledge.

Special thanks to the Veteran's Health Care System, which works helping disabled veterans [such as I] maintain adequae, healthy living through their professional care programs. It was the VA Chapter 31 Vocational Rehabilitation Program, which provided the monetary support for my present educational achievements. All veterans—in one way or the other— who served in the combat return home from the theatre of war with a change in their lives. These veterans are always in need of assistances as to the reintegration into civilian life. Some of us get these "helps" early on, and others like me discover and get these "helps" later in life relating to a veteran's journey and transition. To all of these professionals of the VA Administration, I say—thanks!

This book, *Wrestling In Deep Waters,* is dedicated to my mother, Augustine Jones, who went home last year (2012) at the graceful age of 84. I had written several secular books prior to this book; *Wrestling In Deep Waters* is her here today because my mother before passing made me promise to write also in the arena of religion. My mother believed in education of two regards, "Know God, and Don't Let the Devil Fool you— be it Secular or Religion." —Sherman A. Jones

GENERAL INTRODUCTION

Wrestling In Deep Waters

Recursively, all—in a juxtaposition alongside the knowledge of God—must admit that we do not know very much. This is the way it is, in God, as we wrestle in these deep waters of time and circumstances. This is no different than attempting to know a specific progression of one term to the next —with no knowledge of the elliptical jumping from generalities to specifics—which only "omniscience" can do. God, alone, possesses the attribute of being "omniscience" knowing everything from the end back to the beginning. In our water wrestle of time, juxtaposing our mind beside the mind of God, this is the same as understanding the base clause f (0) = 0, f (n + 1) = f (n) + 3 specifying the successive terms of the sequence f (n) = 3n. Understandably, it is God the three in one as the best of all and everything. God is the only "best" that "better" cannot beat. Allow me to turn back to simplicity, O. K.?

I do not know very much; although, I have a bunch of college degrees. Humbly speaking, my knowledge is elementary, even, with my four degrees. It was July 27, 2013, that I acquired my fourth degree—a "Bachelor's degree in Paralegal Studies;" I graduated "Magna Cum Laude" for an academic level of distinction used by educational institutions to signify an academic degree, which was received "with great honor." I know about as much as a lawyer does, which is still to say, not very much. As a matter of fact, I am the learned person that does most of the lawyers research, writing of memorandums, writing legal briefs, analogizing, and distinguishing case precedents for court cases. In other words, I have skills, but I still do not know very much.

My great-grand-pappy use to say all the time, "A little knowledge is dangerous." I guest this is why the bible says, "Wisdom is the principal thing; therefore get wisdom: and with all thy getting get understanding" (KJV, Pr. 4:7). All a little knowledge and wisdom without an understanding can cause is, just, a drifting down stream to wherever these waters would carry one. This is the way it has been with/for much of humanity, going along with the flow, with the least amount of resistance. When we really think about it, even, it is probable that you know more than me. Would you believe me as to the telling us this, "God does not require us to know a lot"? God's *benchmark* (a point of reference as a decisive factor), relating to human knowledge, is God's principles; whereas, and even, Adam and Eve did not succeed with honors, lost their nobility. "I [says God] will give them a heart to know

Me that I am the LORD, and they shall be My people, and I will be their God, for they shall return to Me with their whole heart" (KJV, Jer. 24:7). This is our regained nobility!

Wrestling In Deep Waters in today's society (secular and religious), these waters are tumultuous, murky, dirty, back stabbing for the almighty dollar. This "wrestle" leaves a worshipper empty, and those outside of worship with lots of money. Then comes death to both. There moneys stay but they depart. Love-ones are left to *Wrestling In Deep Waters* fighting over the departed ill gained wealth. The real mark was missed because real wealth is loving God. We are to "Love God's above gold" (KJV, Psalm 119:127)! The praising of our God, as to his mercy—"in us"—is the breakdown of simplicity. A man, a woman, a boy, or a girl is a trichotomy (a group of three). Scripture says:

> For the word of God is intelligent, powerful, and sharper than any two-edged sword, piercing even to the dividing asunder of "***soul and*** (1) ***spirit***," and of the "***joints and*** (2) ***marrow***," and is a discerner of the "***thoughts and*** (3) ***intents***" of the heart. Neither is there any creature that is not manifest in his sight: but all things are naked and opened unto the eyes of him with whom we have to do we must give account (KJV Heb 4:12-13).

The "1-2-3s" ("soul and spirit," "joints and marrow," "thoughts and intents") are easily explainable:

> The one (1) "***soul and spirit*** is unquestionably "the-you" of whatever you are as a being. This, you (soul and spirit) live in the body but also live with outside the body in an unexplainable dimension called eternity(heaven and hell). Guess what houses the soul and spirit!

> The two (2) "***joints and marrow***"is the functioning cadaver that we have termed the body. This is the present evidence we see in the mirror. "Therefore, says the scripture, we are always confident, knowing that, whilst we are at home in the body, we are absent from the Lord" (KJV 2 Cor. 5:6).

> The three (3) "***thoughts and intents***" is what we call conscientiousness or the mind. There is an extraordinarily compelling argument for this arrangement, which sums up the simplicity of the "1 and 2s.

The "three (3)" (thoughts and intents [=mind]) is as to the design of inherency with everything and everybody: "in the likeness of God"(KJV Genesis. 5:1). This is the same even with computers; whereas, according to WiseGeek (2003-2013) "POP is a protocol for storage of email. [You, do have a one?]

SMTP is a protocol for sending and receiving.[1]

God, in a contradictory statement, "is the similar and the unlikeness of a computer", sends and receives his own word from the storage of his eternal infinity allows humanity access. Accessibility within knowledge is the mind; as, "POP" is of a computer storaging everything that we do in life's encounters: the heard, the imaged, and, even the seen. God's process is the soul (who we are) sends directions through the mind to the body acquires righteous reception, if is of God. The soul sends through the mind, and the body receives. This all sounds simple, and is, is made complex because of our disloyality in the water, with the water. The problem in all of our lives is the erection of no longer being trustworthy. We sure cannot trust our mind, which 24/7 is at work evaluating, comparing, and judging. In these waters we need God, God's thoughts on our person(the soul) is the values that keep us centered. With confident going forward, we are not to get confused *Wrestling In Deep Waters* because we know that "God is not the author of confusion" (1Cor. 14:33).

In these incoming chapters, we will understand God's perspective given to Ezekiel that concludes that God is the only absolute. As to this reading and the

---

[1] Conjucture Corporation. "What is the Difference Between SMTP and POP?" *WiseGeek*. 2003-2013. http://www.wisegeek.com/what-is-the-difference-between-smtp-and-pop.htm (accessed April 21, 2013).

specifics, this is just *"general introduction."* After this *"general introduction,"* there will be an *"introduction's overtures"* leaving chance to nothing. These will be to the defining of the message/messages, which will parlay us to a sameness juxtaposed to text, context, and hopefully to the right interpretation of God's word. This is a must be! The metaphors, connotations, denotations, hyperboles, paradoxes, parodies, modernisms, and postmodernisms are numerous in our 47th chapter of Ezekiel. These impose a "general introduction" and an "intoduction's overtures" lay the foundation for the spiritual erection of God's word climaxing with God on the cross in center of our lives.

As to the all inclusivenes of *"Wrestling In Deep Waters,"* God takes Ezekiel [as God did Paul and many others] to a place we really know not, but is, called "the third heaven"(KJV 2 Cor. 12.2). In this place of "we know not," called "the third heaven," Ezekiel's is here in a, right-now, retroactive true picture perfecting reality of all, past, present, & future. Recently, Baudrillard wrote a piece of literature contrasting modernism and postmodernism looked at history as a retroactive living and stated:

> History is our former referential, that is to express our myth." He goes on to say, "The great event of this period, the great trauma, is this reduction of strong references, these death

pangs of the real and of the rationale that open onto an age of simulation.[2]

Stepping out of character is to be bold, occassionlly, this is where one can make such statement as: God is true reality. "I *'in'* him; and, he *'in'* me; and, you too!" The text of the story introducing this transcendency of the prophet Ezekiel is only a text; and, a still-shot as to the "all and too is still all God." Hello, good morning, somebody! Strong— see? I will do my best, first, refraining from over dramalizations because I want you to enjoy this book with me not on the merit of just emotional excitement.

Here we go, and I am coming at you. The figure of speech, which speaks to the "coming content: "A man with a line in his hand. . ."is featured measuring these waters is within the context of life's religions. Remember, I told you that I know but little! I cannot answer definitely how God takes a man. This is above my "pay grade!" This was Mr. Obama's answer when was asked, "When is a fetus considered a person?" "Above my pay grade!" Do you know that he was correct and gave the proper answer. I l proving of almost everthing that I say. Listen with me to what God say to us through Jermiah when it comes to birth,

[2] BAUDRILLARD, JEAN. "I: On Postmodernity." Modules on Baudrillard. n.d. Felluga, Dino. "Modules on Baudrillard: On Postmodernity." Introductory Guide to Critical Theory. Date of last update, which you can find on the home page. Purdue U. Date you accessed the site. <http://www.purdue.edu/guidetotheory/postmodernism/modules/ba (accessed April 4, 2013).

"Before I formed thee in the belly I knew thee, and before thou camest forth out of the womb I sanctified thee, and I ordained thee a prophet unto the nations"(KJV Jer 1:5). After that stated, I can give you parts of what I call **"the mix."** Evangelism, gospel preaching, and teaching with a growth's paradox, these waters of life have risen quite high. I believe I can pause and say, "The world is quite crowded with many strange understandings out of and in these troubling waters."

I am not trying to reintroduce God to you nor part par-excellence in your mind as to the person of God. I only know God for myself as my "Chief Cornerstone," and the foundation upon which I stand. As always, I have endeavored—according to the dictates of scripture, "Feed the flock of God which is among you, taking the oversight thereof, not by constraint, but willingly; , not for filthy lucre, but of a ready mind" (KJV1 Peter 5:2). With God and of the spirit, it is this view of being accepted by God that positions us as characters on the world's stage as part of the cast in God's eternal picture show, *Wrestling In Deep Waters.*

The entertainment begins with Ezekiel *Wrestling In Deep Waters.* Living frames our works giving all credit and "everything back to God." God determines before "time" all roles we play in God's universal picture show. We (as a character) are [as I think with my little knowledge] in this universal picture show acting out the part/parts that God so designed just for us. God wrote the script that covers all of humanity's existence and vented it into a picture show. God's commanding scene is strong letting us know only in part our part as we wait for another part after *"Wrestling in Deep Waters."*

Each chapter of Ezekiel's prophetic book is but a flicker picture frame. Ezekiel is not given any more than what he/we need to know. If, Ezekiel were given further; there might be no need to trust God. Since Ezekiel, like us, knows not the mind of God, we can only trust God and take God at his word. "I will not leave you comfortless: I will come to you" (KJV, Jn 14:18). Whatever we think we know is only a little and nothing without and beyond God. God is "the author and finisher of our faith." This is what the preacher said about God and our little: "He hath made every thing beautiful in his time: also he hath set the world in their heart so that no man can find out the work that God maketh from the beginning to the end" (KJV, Ecc. 3:11).

Let us not forget this book of Ezekiel is compiled for "the inhabitant of God's Kingdom." Ezekiel book has forty-eight (48) chapters extending to us forty-eight (48) pictures. The Academy-Award Oscar goes to—— Ezekiel's "Valley of Dry Bones." With the fast forward remote from the "Valley of Dry Bones," we are here in Ezekiel chapter forty-seven (47).

God, the producer, is working the best in us contrary to Hollywood. Hollywood does the reverse: ask any actor or actress. Hollywood works the best out of an actor/actress; and in some instances, leave the actor/actress in such a state until even the dogs do not want them. You know, "Dogged Out!" God is the most excellent; he does the opposite, in said, "He lifts us higher and higher." God inspires us out of ourselves and puts himself back into us—as he did with Ezekiel.

In the coming together with God's word, the waters and words are synonymous. The profundity is within the metaphorical. This metaphor (water) is the word, which gives an insight of the connoted allegory. God in man's knowledge and understanding directs the artistry of the declared. "And all the people went their way to eat and drink, to send portions and rejoice exceedingly, because they understood the words that were declared to them" (Ne 8:12). The encompassed understanding is in the eaten up as part of being measured and cannot be isolated from humanity allows humans to suffer with the "Tares and Wheat," in these metaphorical waters. God burned in scripture, starting with Ezekiel chapter one, his word, which came to Ezekiel expressed in each chapter that he has not nor will never forsake us.

Here, now in chapter 47; we have it, and all we need to know is that God "brought me again. . .!'"

Within the received advance contract which God extends to us, God has never been a negative, neither is "Wheat." Metaphorically, the God of waters is the wheat, which = God's word. Tares become mixed in these waters cause us our wrestle, which are Satan and man's word planted among God's word. In the context of being metaphorical, the word, "Water," in and of God is the simile, the imagery, and the figure of speech to the directing of God's children to his "good." The truth of the beginning word of/from God, there is no end. Here is a serious lick, from the bible: "The beginning of strife is as when one letteth out water..." (Prov. 17:14). This refers to the Devil, and the watering down of God's word spoken by men. God is three in one, which is one, but Satan is one by one; whereas, the Devil will never be equal with God. Along the way, in the way, and of the way, the story we are reading points back to God, and God alone. "God trumps the Devil."

What is most fascinating—the past and the present have much the same similarities as to an involvement. God is still God! As we look forward, let us not get tied down in controversies of the feeble-minded of the having you to believe that man is only 4,000 years old as if Africans were not humans. Skeletonal remains of Africans predates and have been discovered to exist over "4 million years . . . ."[3] As the little boy says in the hood, "The Devil got game." The Devil is a lie, and the Devil is still the Devil; just as, water is still water. As we all know, life is filled with a combination of good and of evil (Wheat and Tares). I like what Dr. King said, "He who passively accepts evil is as much involved in it as he who helps to perpetrate it. He who accepts evil without protesting against it is cooperating with it."[4] To the much and the most, this sums it up. Right? This is to some the dialectically definition, which is defined by the contrasted.

However, the continuous flowing pond became polluted, and there is only an allowing solution as *"Tares and Wheat,"* are mixed in our daily lives. Here is shouting News! A day of separation is around the "bend." Just Wheat; Tares no more! Separation is the evidence of God's sovereignty over everything connotes the reliability of his word. In the far-

---

[3] Shreeve, Jamie. "Ardi Surrounded by Family." *National Geographic News.* October 28, 2010. http://news.nationalgeographic.com/news/2009/10/091001-oldest-human-skeleton-ardi-missing-link-chimps-ardipithecus-ramidus.html (accessed April 3, 2013).

[4] Leadershipwithyou. "Martin Luther King Junior Leadership Case Study." Leadership With You. 2008–2013. http://www.leadership-with-you.com/martin-luther-king-junior-leadership.html (accessed March 29, 2013).

reached transitional of God, the "far" is the "near."
Ezekiel found this out.   You do know this, don't
you?   "Beware of dogs, beware of evil workers,
beware of the concision" (KJV Phil. 3:2).   These
are they who polluted the water sowing "tares"
among the "wheat." "Tares," using acceptable truths,
slanted by man serving the Devil. His is not the word
of God!   Tares are Devil's words, which give the
impression of being God's word, which cause death,
which offers nothing to the living. The scripture says,
"The beginning of the words of his mouth is
foolishness: and   the   end   of   his   talk   is
mischievous   madness" (KJV Ecc. 10:13).   This
"Wrestling In Deep Waters is the combined word
that causes   struggle in our daily lives. "Tares
and Wheat" as the pendulum swings in the dividing
of the right from the wrong for us on our pilgrimage
journey waits a day of separation.

    We sojourn in the joining of the prophets and
Ezekiel as they wrestle in their waters. God is about
to do something right now in our lives.   Here, we
are—away from and out of mind—grazing upon the
revealed glory of God's heart and is humbled after the
resurrection. God's word is in the expanded; here is
victorious despite the "growth factor" that allowed
the swollen influxed hyperboles.   These are the
Tares, and these are the "Tares" prepared for
separation will be burned in hell's fire.   The long-
suffering we must endure will be rewarded at the point

of separating the tares from the wheat. The separation is the Lord to perform.

Keeping all things real, life's difficulties are God's opportunities to instill further growth in our lives. His authority over his creations and creatures is in the assigned responsibility of himself. Ezekiel in these faith water is humbled. At the river where God transcends man, God can do everything accept transcend himself. This means that God can do whatever, but will not do whatever. Therefore, in the capsule of all things, God's chooses not to do "the whatever" keeps God, God!

As we see, there is a bigger picture; whereas, our visions are just as clear as was Ezekiel's vision. Don't let go of your umbrella! Why is the question, which asks another questions that begs an answer. What do you, or can you say to God other than, thanks? In a deliberative attempt to know the answer to the question reqires more questions. Is this the beginning or is this the ending statement? I am of a further opinion—referring to beginning and ending with God, they are relatively the same. "The thing that hath been, it is that which shall be; and that which is done is that which shall be done: and there is no new thing under the sun" (KJV, Ecc 1:9). As a show of everything, God is planting his seed (his word) in our spirit for a delivery, and this word once delivered into humanity will not return unto him void. God metaphorically spoke to us from ancient times referenced to the "Tares and the Wheat" this way, " Instead of the thorn shall come up—the fir tree, and instead of the brier shall come up—the myrtle tree: and it shall be to the LORD for a name, for an everlasting sign that shall not be cut off" (Isa 55: 13).

Wrestling In Deep Waters in the paradox of evangelicism's growth "Tares and Wheat" are the mixed "good and evil" spoken in words to deeds. It is here God allows his living to continue as, "He maketh his sun to rise on the evil and on the good, and sendeth rain on the just and on the unjust"(Matt 5:45). It is great injustice and tragedy to give away God's power that was once given to you. Satan will accept anything that you are will to give up because without yours he has nothing. Down the ages, there have been much unwanted seeds planed among the wheat, and the evil seed seducers are still seducing, making muddy these spiritual waters that have travelled times pathway.

Evangelically, the word of God continues to grow with a mixture of "Tare and Wheat." The days before Ezekiel, the days during Ezekiel, and the days after Ezekiel should be the days of no surprises. The word says, "Let no man deceive himself. If any man among you seemeth to be wise in this world, let him become a fool, that he may be wise" (1 Cor 3:18).

God's word is so correct until it interprets itself in our understanding. The word says, "There is a spirit in man: and the inspiration of the Almighty giveth them understanding" (Job 32:8). Let us now journey a little further on up the king's highway into the book of Ezekiel the 47th chapter, which will strip us all bare. We might as well unveil ourself becasue scripture says, "All things are naked and opened unto the eyes of him with whom we have to do" (KJV, Heb 4:13).

Base Text Guiding The Writing Process

These are following text of scriptures, which highlight the composition of this book **Ezekiel 47:1-7**:

1. *Afterward he brought me again unto the door of the house; and, behold, waters issued out from under the threshold of the house eastward: for the forefront of the house stood toward the east, and the waters came down from under from the right side of the house, at the south side of the altar* (Ezekiel 47:1).

2. *Then brought he me out of the way of the gate northward, and led me about the way without unto the utter gate by the way that looketh eastward; and,*

behold, there ran out waters on the right side. (KJV, Ezekiel 47:2).

3. *And when the man that had the line in his hand went forth eastward, he measured a thousand cubits, and he brought me through the waters; the waters were to the ankles.* (KJV, Ezekiel 47:3).

4. *Again he measured a thousand, and brought me through the waters; the waters were to the knees. Again he measured a thousand, and brought me through; the waters were to the loins.* (KJV, Ezekiel 47:4).

5. *Afterward he measured a thousand; and it was a river thatI could not pass over: for the waters were risen, waters to swim in, a river that could not be passed over.* (KJV, Ezekiel 47:5).

6. *And he said unto me, Son of man, hast thou seen this? Then he brought me, and caused me to return to the brink of the river.* (KJV, Ezekiel 47:6).

7. *Now when I had returned, behold, at the bank of the river were very many trees on the one side and on the other.* (KJV, Ezekiel 47:7).

The beginning was of purity with God releasing himself from an overflow in every nook and cranny of humanity's resolve. Accept him! God has given all of humanity a "free agency." The crescendo of Dr. King (1968) still resounds anew as he spoke back, when:

Like anybody, I would like to live a long life. Longevity has its place. But I'm not concerned about that now. I just want to do God's will. And He's allowed me to go up to the mountain. And I've looked over. And I've seen the Promised Land. I may not get there with you. But I want you to know tonight, that we, as a people, will get to the promised land (para. 1).[5]

[5] The New York Times: Dr. King. *Martin Luther King Jr.* January 15, 2013. http://topics.nytimes.com/topics/reference/timestopics/people/k/martin_luthe r_jr_king/index.html (accessed January 15, 2013).

The Biblical Dispensations

The rest is covered in our text of Scriptures [after our introduction's overtures] will focus upon the seven dispensations [God's biblical periods of time], which is of God with a man living there from. The seven dispensations are as follows according to Scofield:[6]

1. Man's innocent: See Gen. 1:26; Gen. 2:16,17; Gen. 3:6; Gen. 3:22-24.)

2. Man under conscience: See Gen. 3:7, 22; Gen. 6:5,11-12; Gen. 7:11-12, 23.)

3. Man in authority over the earth: (See Gen. 9: 1, 2; Gen. 11: 1-4; Gen. 11:5-8.)

4. Man under promise: (See Gen. 12:1-3; Gen. 13:14-17; Gen. 15:5; Gen. 26:3; Gen. 28: 12-13; Exod. 1: 13-14.)

5. Man under the law: (See Exod. 19:1-8; 2 Kings 17:1-18; 2 Kings 25: 1 -11; Acts 2:22-23; Acts 7:5152; Rom. 3:19-20; Rom. 10:5; Gal. 3: 10.)

---

[6] Scofield, C I. "THE SEVEN DISPENSATIONS." *Biblecentre.org* . October 28, 2006. http://www.biblecentre.org/topics/cis_rd_2_seven_disp.htm (accessed April 4, 2013).

6. Man under grace: (See Luke 17:26-30; Luke 18:8; 2 Thess. 2:7-12; Rev. 3:15-16.) (See Jer. 30:5-7; Dan. 12:1; Zeph. 1:15-18; Matt. 24:21-22.)

7. Man under the personal reign of Christ: (See Isa. 2:1-4; Isa. 11; Acts 15:14-17; Rev. 19: 11-21; Rev. 20:1-6. (See Rev. 20:3,7-15; Rev. 21 and 22.).

Wrestling In Deep Waters context of word will relegate notable sub-legs under/within every dispensation without compromising God's word and the rules of correlation. Have we heard that all good things come in threes? Me too! There are many heathens disguising themselves as good. What is being said for our understanding is that God added human interchange to the somewhat lackluster subject of dispensations.

1. This leg "in the order" as a secondary has to do with the testing of man. This testing was before the sowing of the first offensive seed (tares). "And the LORD God commanded the man, saying, Of every tree of the garden thou mayest freely eat: But of the tree of the knowledge of good and evil, thou shalt not eat of it: for in the day that thou eatest thereof thou shalt surely die" (KJV Ge 2:16-17). These tests are not saying that God does not what we are going to do; on the contrary, these tests are saying we

need find out what we are going to do.   God already knows!

2. Secondly, this dispensation's manifested notable second sub-leg is "our failures or inability to obey the prescribed by God.   In other words, we broke the law!   All things considered and, however, the law was but a schoolmaster in the first place. "Therefore, the law was our schoolmaster to bring us unto Christ that we might be justified by faith" (KJV" Gal 3:24).

3. Finally, God is a just-judge.   As a third sub-leg, each dispensation extends to us a divine judgment for our failures to keep the commandments of God.   "For neither they who are circumcised keep the law, but desire to have you circumcised that they may glory in your flesh" (KJV Gal 6:13).   Let us not be dismayed because each dispensation as to the sub-legs are mirror images of each other.   The Swelling is a growing continual into the final dispensation. For now, it is with spiritual acknowledgement that, "5 For John truly baptized with water, but ye shall be baptized with the Holy Ghost not many days hence" (KJV Acts 1:5).

Despite the entertaining, the ultimate gives God glory.   These above dispensations will get an inclusion in the chapters to follow. However, these will not overshadow God's word of "joy." In these, there will be much swelling because of the "tares" that have been mixed with the "wheat." Nonetheless, this information could have been the "preface." Reaching forward, the river on the other shore excites, gives joy, and will not bog us down with a saturated doctrine killing the spirit. Here is the shout going forward, the scripture says, "And by the river upon the bank thereof, on this side and on that side, shall grow all trees for meat, whose leaf shall not fade, neither shall the fruit thereof be consumed: it shall bring forth new fruit according to his months, because their waters they issued out of the sanctuary: and the fruit thereof shall be for meat, and the leaf thereof for medicine" (KJV, Eze 47:12). These dispensational inclusions will be combined into five time segments for simplification, only. A thorough exegesis of these dispensations will not be in the taking away or demeaning the glory of God. As spoken by Pau, I say the same, "Finally, brethren, pray for us that the word of the Lord may have free course, and be glorified, even as it is with you" (KJV2 Thess 3:1).

Range of Bible Chapters

Schemes	Genesis 1–3	Genesis 3–8	Genesis 9–11	Genesis 12 to Exodus 19	Exodus 20 to Acts 1	Acts 2 to Revelation 20	Revelation 20:4-6	Revelation 20–22
or 8 Dispensational cheme	Innocence or Edenic	Conscience or Antediluvian	Civil Government	Patriarchal or Promise	Mosaic or Law	Grace or Church	Millennial Kingdom	Eternal State or Final
Dispensational cheme	Patriarchal				Mosaic	Ecclesial	Zionic	
Dispensational cheme (minimalist)	Law					Grace	Kingdom	

FIELD'S CONTINUUM

Introduction's Overtures

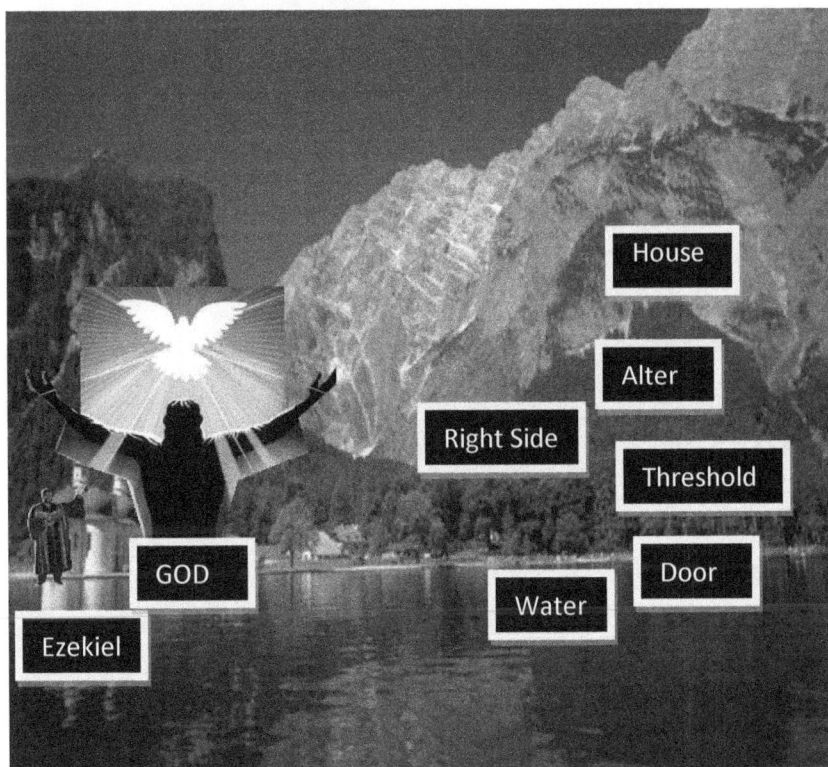

Afterward he brought me again unto the door of the house; and, behold, waters issued out from under the threshold of the house eastward: for the forefront of the house stood toward the east, and the waters came down from under from the right side of the house, at the south side of the altar (KJV Ezekiel 47:1).

Then brought he me out of the way of the gate northward, and led me about the way without unto the utter gate by the way that looketh eastward; and, behold, there ran out waters on the right side. (KJV, Ezekiel 47:2).

The Simplistic Inspection

I've learned in living, after have lived a minute or two, that you cannot always believe everything you hear. It is looking at the entire field of life that I will say, "It's a vast field," and the "water continue to rise and swell," but the gnat gets no bigger.

My great-grand-pappy was never schooled. He was wise, in his own mind, as to everything he told me. By the creek fishing or in the cotton field with great-grand-pappy, I was told many tales. I accept most of what my old great-grand-pappy told me, "back then." Let me say this, no matter if my grand-pappy was right or wrong; even today, I still remember everything. Much of what he said has taken me from yonder to this point on my journey. I must admit everything my great-grand-pappy said sounded convincing. Here's just one example: "Believe none of that which you hear; and-only, half that you see." I am not ashamed of my age, but let it suffice as to the before-stated, "I am old schooler, and my communication with my grand-pappy was in the cotton fields." In the cotton field, I would pray for rain. I wanted the water to come. Not realizing I was getting the word. My grand-pappy was carrying me through the waters all the while. I believe that he knew that these waters, over time, will become deeper than these old cotton fields, which will prove my old grand pappy right in some regards. *Wrestling In Deep Waters,* as my old grand-pappy would say, "It's hell in deep waters if you are not in the boat."

As an overture, whether you know it or not, there is still, even in and here, some cotton picking going on in, in "The Fields' Continuum." For Jesus said, "Behold, I say to you, lift up your eyes and look at the fields, for they are already white for harvest" (KJV Jn 4:35)! But, Beware! There will be some "Tares" among the "Wheat." These same tares that disguise themselves as wheat is what make clean water dirty. It is in the going forward that "The Fields' Continuum" nearing harvest time, according Jesus must, "Let both (tares and wheat) grow together until the harvest"(KJV, Mt 13:30).

No matter how we look at it, or how we think about it—cotton fields or not—all belong to God, and all have a type of life's wrestles in one way or another. I genuinely like the ease in writing this book as I come with us, Wrestling In Deep Waters. This is easy writing because much of everything that I say to you I have personal experience in the living of life. I know about stubbon weeds (Tares) in the crop. This is nothing new because I have chopped many these weeds from around the cotton and the corn, in the field. Personally, in my life, God has had to do a lot of forgiving to let me live this long, and you too. It is here in the continuum of life that I better understand what my "Old Grand Pappy" was trying to get me to understand. With a little education and a little bit of living, it is clearer as we put education in our living experiences, we cannot believe all things that come out of the mouth of man. With perceptive and from times to times, one can only believe "some," and at other times, "the all," and then at further times, "the none." The last part of what my "Old Grand Pappy" said is always true, "Believe only half that you see." Least that I'll never forget! God has the final say, and some things just have to grow together. This doesn't mean that we have to take for granted any and everything. All things are not ever all practical; however, the incorrect word sown into our developmental progress (on the journey) we call them "Tares." As to the fruit of our labor and the fertile, we call—in/for the preparation of going to the next in this "The Fields' Continuum" and beyond—"Wheat."

God from his kind nature wants us excited herein with his manna and joy. God's droppings of generosity extend from heaven's throne split the crevices of our lives as we eat the "Showbread." "And when the dew fell upon the camp in the night, the manna fell upon it" (KJV, Nu 11:9). We are never too late to experience his joy nor too early to celebrate within his victory. The happiness is in the "forever bread" that another cannot take away. And Jesus said, "This is that bread, which came down from heaven; not as your fathers did eat manna, and are dead: he that eateth of this bread shall live forever" (KJV John 6:58). As 'to the hearing the rest of the story,' "I am," exclaimed Jesus, "the bread of life: he that cometh to me shall never hunger" (KJV John 6:35).

As a juxtaposition, "Jesus" and "manna" are one with there being no "tares" mixed in either, just wheat, sweat and wet. These waters are—clean and clear —not that deep at all, and, if so, with Jesus, as was with Peter, we can walk with the Master on these waters. Jesus knows about our sometimes emptiness, this is why; it is written, "These things have I spoken unto you, that my joy might remain in you and that your joy might be full" (KJV John 15:12). Before going to the pinnacle of the mountain top, let's us not forget that "Wheat" is God's Holy bread. "*Wrestling In Deep Waters*" is the meeting on the inside, and the "Tares are the enemy's deeds. As to "Wheat" both the baker and the stomach rejoice; for, there is no longer a want, and our needs are full of joy.

The unhappy, the cynical, and the sowers of the "tares" have attempted to poisoned supply of waters. Tares in the "wheat" create disbelief, which

shafts and fleeces the flock of God. Believe me—
you. Having a degree in law, I know Pharisees. In
our spiritual environments and churches, we are
plagued with "Pharisees" even today, which
operates from their logos questioning everything.
With no faith in service and after service, these
walk away empty with no joy. Not long ago, I
read this an article by Morton (1999), which stated:

> Many Fundamentalists when confronted with
> the term "legalism" (or legalist") quickly insist it
> only applies to lost people who seek salvation by
> works of the law. Though it can mean this,
> "legalism" is not limited to this narrow definition
> as any dictionary can attest. A more common
> and accepted term among Bible believers for
> groups that teach salvation by works is
> "cult" instead of "legalism." The Jehovah's
> Witnesses, Christian Scientists, Mormons, and
> other groups who teach salvation by works are
> routinely known as "a cult (Morton 1999)[7]

Understandably and admittably, history
does not record everything. In most instances, the
written piece of history is hard to refute—both the
traditional and the extraordinary. However, as a point

---

[7] Morton, Timothy S. "Chapter I: Legalism Verses Liberty." From Liberty to
Legalism. 1999. http://www.biblebelievers.com/Morton_legalism-liberty.html
(accessed March 8, 2013).

of emphasis, God is before history. Allow me to go back to my old grand-pappy, O. K.? He could neither read nor write; but, you could not cheat him out of a dime. Life's dual dimensions of good and evil, more than anything, has in the growth exercise of worship allowed tares and wheat to grow together. I don't know who is "Saved or is not Saved," and neither you. I am of the position when we get to wherever we are going; we all are going to be surprised as to who is going to be standing next to us. See, if this can help us, Jesus said, "There came a certain poor widow, and she threw in two mites, who make a farthing. And he called unto him his disciples, and saith unto them, Verily I say unto you, That this poor widow hath cast more in, than all they which have cast into the treasury: For all they did cast in of their abundance; but she of her want did cast in all that she had, even all her living" (KJV Mark 12:42-44).

There is "a confirmation of opinions or a variation of opinions" as with almost everything, which has tried its way over into our spiritual experiences. These are they that have troubled our waters. Of Course, it is essential for us to look at this complex picture understanding the genres of religions. The crucifix came with the usage of God's word as the water flowed from the altar to the river with man's religion and complicity. *"Wrestling In Deep Waters"* is the here in of the river where we all shake of the tares before crossing over the Jordan to the other side.

With the little that we know, it seems as if Ezekiel has gotten lost in the mix, just as most of us, leaving the way from time to time. Someone said the other day, "I am not the only human!" I can accept this excuse rather than the pious, "Holy than thou attitude of some of us." This is how the lost among us feel. I must strive to be careful and not go ahead of these old flowing waters. You do know that these waters are flowing? It is here that most years—than not—that the Jordon river swells around harvest time. "And as they that bore the ark were come unto the Jordan, and the feet of the priests that bore the ark dipped in the edge of the water, (for the Jordan overflows all its banks all the time of harvest)" (KJV Joshua 3: 15). It is here where the word of God in the annals of time grows, but the watering of "Wheat" also waters the "tares." Remember, the priests do not have the power to establish nor the ability to measure these waters. Only "the man with the line in his hand" can measures these waters sees man's words leaving so many unfilled, disappointed, and surprise.

These waters, these words, are mixed with tares and wheat, as the journey of Ezekiel continues. Herein, the flowing of these waters [these words] has for us potentially irreversible consequences. It is at present in the evolution of religion man has used God's word in many fashionable directions. His word disguised by the use of witchcraft and slight of hand. It is in those cult-like manner using rhetorical persuasions, by man, allows evil a designed purpose to flourish. Behind the non-sacred veil, there is a veil of secrecy that permeates among the members of those certain sects. Among these are "clouds and a codes of silence." "And GOD saw that the wickedness of man was great in the earth and that every imagination of the thoughts of his heart was only evil continually" (KJV Genesis 6:5). Wickedness is no new phenomena; and if were, I presume there would be a jaw dropping "awe," an all out shock. Even, in the days, of the Genesis story, there were accounts; imagine now, how insane some of our religions—or should I say religious leaders— are in the much to with nothing, and yet, seemingly, infecting everyone today. The scripture says, "Evil men and seducers shall wax worse and worse, deceiving, and being deceived" (KJV, 2Tim 3:13).

Wrestling in Deep Waters with the influxes of *Evangelical Growth's Paradox* as a subtext is the interpretations of God's word—placing "tares" among the "wheat"— is saturated with the hyperboles of evil. These exaggerated pitches of man—in the usage of God's word— are the players choice in the receiving benefits perceived of their own hypocritical satisfactions.   Not just of Ezekiel's day, but every day from the "near dawn of man" to the man of this present day and age.   We love looking into antiquity as a mean of "shifting;" as if, sin do not rest at our door the same.   And, Jesus said:

> For judgment I am come into this world, that they which see not might see; and that they which see might be made blind. And some of the Pharisees which were with him heard these words, and said unto him, Are we blind also? Jesus said unto them, If ye were blind, ye should have no sin: but now ye say, We see; therefore your sin remaineth (KJV Jn 9:39-41).

The Israelites—like all races from one time to another experienced slavery—their country had enemies on all sides, and they were conquered and carried into bondage. Do you not know, this is still possible even today, if there is not a watchman to sound the alarm?   Ezekiel needs this interview with God for confidence. Ezekiel was a true prophet of God and did not use exaggerations in the lord-ing over his people. Yet, Ezekiel was responsible for the messaging.   Why?   Read   the   following   for understanding:

> So thou, O son of man, I have set thee a watchman unto the house of Israel; therefore thou shalt hear the word at my mouth, and warn

them from me. When I say unto the wicked, O wicked man, thou shalt surely die; if thou dost not speak to warn the wicked from his way, that wicked man shall die in his iniquity; but his blood will I require at thine hand. Nevertheless, if thou warn the wicked of his way to turn from it; if he do not turn from his way, he shall die in his iniquity; but thou hast delivered thy soul (KJV, Eze 33:7-9).

Today the word is growing but is full of hyperbole. McCarthy & Carter (2003) looked at these hyperboles and stated in a description:

> The listeners' reactions depend crucially to the interpretations and the successes of hyperboles on the listeners entering a pact of acceptance of extreme formulations, the creation of impossible worlds, and/or apparent counterfactuality.[8]

As a follow-up, every religious or doctrine within a religion's beginning has a source. It is the belief of some leader that is always an emotional hypochondriac that uses exaggerations to make persons obedient to his sickness or his insanity.

---

[8] McCarthy, Michael & Carter, Ronald. ""There's millions of them":
hyperbole in everyday conversation." *ScienceDirect*. 2003.
http://www.sciencedirect.com/science/article/pii/S0378216603001164
(accessed January 13, 2013).

"Hyperboles" are exaggerations, overstatements, embellishments, and escalations, which attempts to destroy the glory of God's word. This is the paradox associated with evangelical growth. It is in the seeing man becomes earthly powerful until he too will almost do, say, or exhort to any measure in the maintaining of his superiority. It is the boldness of the human animal that puts religion at the forefront of their existence. It is in man's beliefs that have manifested themselves in all that is humanity. Jesus warns, "Beware of false prophets, which come to you in sheep's clothing, but inwardly they are ravening wolves" (KJV Mt 7:15).

The paradox inconsistencies of men have created a bloom mixed of "tares" with God's word. These tares produced/produces many religions under different names. Here is the biggest paradox of all: In most instances they all tend to succeed no matter the name. These are in the likeness of God's Word—at the altar—with their own standards and, often times, frightening substances. These religions are numerous: Alternative Religions, Anglicanism, Baha'I, Buddhism, Catholicism, Christianity, Latter-day Saints, Healing, Hinduism, Islam, Jehovah's Witnesses, Judaism, New Age, Pagan/Wiccan Religion, Protestantism, or Atheism and they all have their many followers. These religions are all designed by self differences making themselves different from the other with knowing exaggerations.

The augmentation within their growth as a paradox feeds [tares among wheat] upon the unsuspecting sacrifices for its self survival as a snake creeps through the night pounces upon its prey. This travel of man's word is the abuse in the *"The Evangelistic Growth's Paradox,"* which has cause to this *"Wrestling In Deep Waters.* The word says as to this wrestling, "For we wrestle not against flesh and blood, but against principalities, against powers, against the rulers of the darkness of this world, against spiritual wickedness in high places" (KJV, Eph 6:12).

No matter how stupid and crazy a leader or how silly and bizarre the church, these manage to survive and thrive. It is of scripture concerning the tares and wheat, which says, "Let both grow together until the harvest" (KJV Matt 13:30). However, it is now whence come wars, the believers of each these religions from the histrionics are players acting out cult-like characteristics as the world's product of conflicts. Here Jesus says, "But when ye shall hear of wars and commotions, be not terrified: for these things must first come to pass; but the end is not by and by" (KJV Luke 21:9).

God in pre-adventure is showing us a lot as we

adventure further into the book of Ezekiel. It is within experience that Ezekiel reveals to us the growing of the tares among the wheat. "The man with a line in his hand measuring these waters" share with us waters grow when you put another liquid into the water. God word has always been travelling picks up the debris. This added debris is man's word that mixes with the word of God that grows and deepens the faith waters.

We notice a few more straightforward things; in particular, any and everything can become a religion. Some leaders went and are not sent! There are those leaders that twists the tongue that flips using whatever art of persuasion available for the fleecing of the flock. This is why there is a paradox associated with growth. The religions of man throughout history have caused bleeding of tears quenching thirsty mother earth in an ongoing campaign toward "Revelations' Execution." Man's gorgeous and captivating religions are the rebellions of God's word. It is God's word, which connotes on one hand God's unfailing power.

No matter the power within the designed message of man, God's word will still prevail. This might read as if this is the book; not at all, this is but the introduction's overture that gets us ready for the book.

Regardless, the introduction, introduction's overture, or/and the book of "the-which," the subsequent alignment determines for all a final fate. This final fate will be either one of "eternal life" or one of an "eternal damnation." Herein is a problem. This has not only created untold numbers of religions, but this has also created numerous denominations within each and every religion. All religions believe that they are the only real religion; thus and thereof, each believes that they have a corner market on heaven and has the right to give to others hell that they do not take for themselves.

Looking at the various religions created with "tares and wheat, " the question to ask is: Who is your God is a juxtaposition the near same as asking, who is your mama? Because if your mama is not my mama, you are doomed because my mama's God will decide the faith of all of you. This means all of you, the **Trillions of People** that this world have known and will know before there be time no more, are all doomed. You are doomed because they do not have the one mama of the "who is your mama, fight." Well, my mama is gone and is in some cold grave waiting her resurrection, but mama says...

Defining religion in the most lights, man's reality and acceptance is as to his self identity, which suggest, "Religion is something or that of some enormous importance to a person"[9] (i.e. Football game, basketball game, politics, gambling —yes, even the church or Christianity, and the evils of conservatism). Religions are the stubbornness of the tares and wheat, which allow dogmas to worship by lovers thereof as a creed. I believe this is why in our Ezekiel narrative with "the man with the line in his hand," God ushered Ezekiel out the door for a true experience and a look at himself. Most of our problems with religion is that our religions never get out of the door to be tested. It is here where most religions get their benefits as defined dogmas (behind the door) using the particularities to differentiate themselves from others, which is sad.

From the hood, there is a fixed saying, "The only thing that is certain is death and taxes. This too has gotten into the waters as those in the "hood" too is certainly *Wrestling in Deep Waters* for survival. However, in the life of the saint, a day can make a difference in the dawning. We see and have seen the rise and fall of nations, change within cultures, oppositions just for the sake of saying "no;" with no doubt, the bottom has reached the mountain top. In America, as with other coun-

---

9 Dictionary.com. Word Dictionary. 2013.
http://dictionary.reference.com/browse/religion (accessed January 8, 2013).

tries, we are experiencing and celebrating whites and blacks as equals after the most evil religious background that any country can ever experience. Predominately, the churches of southern America majored in the use of "hyperboles" (overstatements & understatements [Tares]) making their religions a lie to the nation. Misstated the scripture to the making the color of one skin God's curse as being one the biggest lies ever told. Even history will point to the fact that "life came out of Africa and not life in Africa as a beginning." Logic being, if Ham was black, since, he and his brothers had the same father and mother; we would have to conclude that Noah and his wife were "black." You just have to know your history (e.g. Queen Charlotte, wife of the English King George III (1738-1820), was directly descended from Margarita de Castro y Sousa, a black branch of the Portuguese Royal House). The southern slaves did not get this information. I wonder what would have happened if they did? There are many that do not want you to question religion or anything else, and I say to us: question everything, and questioning is good.

When we accept just anything in the name of religion the internal memos of and within religions will turn itself against itself not wanting to win with Christ. The hierarchy within religion preaches equality but do not allow equality. The motivation is one where God is not my God; unless, he allows me to be the ruler over all others.   Those possessed with demons believes that "Hell is better if I have to share Heaven with another of another kind's religion."   Pathetic, you say! Sure, but, this is the mindset of so many, and this is why there are so many Tares among the Wheat.

Hyperboles [Tares] make the self-indulgent of religion selfish in an embedded dominance. This is what allowed the mindset of a "never-was" into existence.   The flowing word of God tells us, "Let your moderation be known unto all men. The Lord is at hand"(KJV, Phil 4:5).   Yet, there are so many still in America adopting the conservatism of the old southern slavery mentality —the use of, or a system based on, using the enforced labor of other people—as a framework under religious ignorance. The word of God in no wise supported neither America's plantation owners nor their descendants, which now lifts their eyes up from hell.   The Three-Fifths Compromise, (is not a constitutional amendment), was an agreement to count three-fifths of a "state's slaves" in apportioning Representatives, Presidential election, and direct taxes. There was never any "Three-Fifth Man" as slavery suggested, and some religious conservatives yet advocate.   Don't fall for the trick of the Devil who want you to believe that he does not exist. The Devil is alive and still lying. He isin congress saying "NO" to God's people, and he is still working the same old "NO" good that he has always been up too down through the ages. This is all in the devils and demons DNA. Religions with these hyperboles echoes in a self-indulgent attempting to control the world with a self-righteousness that rejected God. Some knows; this is the difference between the "went and the sent."

Wrestling In Deep Waters, without a doubt, has mercy hanging in the balance, giving us constantly another chance. Without a mistake, the world looms with the decadence of corruption, and deceit having many gods slaving others to evil. Ask Ezekiel as Go takes Ezekiel to this "Third Heaven" to view all live to come was too a in captivity. As to the spoken, it has been said:

> The high places that were before Jerusalem, which were on the right hand of the mount of corruption, which Solomon the king of Israel had built for Ashtoreth the abomination of the Zidonians, and for Chemosh the abomination of the Moabites, and for Milcom the abomination of the children of Ammon, did the king defile (KJV, Kings 23:13).

With the loss of the way, man's hyperboles [Tares] fashion themselves for sleeping people creates more religions. These religions themselves become a man's god," which points back to the ridiculous. Ezekiel, in our narrative, is focal point of God's words as we follow "the man with line in his hand" in the measuring of these faith's waters pointing to man's sinfulness. This is why the scripture says, "Eyes are full of adultery that cannot cease from sin; beguiling unstable souls: a heart they have exercised with covetous practices; cursed children: Which have forsaken the right way, and are gone astray..." (KJV 2 Peter 2:14-15).

The self-indulged built their wealth supplying itching ears with hyperboles [Tares] captured in their own nefarious and sinful reputations. These occurrences dulled the audience's ears, which in turn nullifies the glory of God from their hearts. "For this people's heart is waxed gross, and their ears are dull of hearing, and their eyes they have closed" (KJV Matt 13:15). Tares and wheat are the result of "The Paradox of Evangelism's Growth" that cause the worship foriegn gods. These paints God's sky with a determinable preference contrary to the blue thereof. The demons and devils are always working to strike a chord of discontent [planting tares] in the spirits of the believers as a split in God's word for the splitting up of God's beauty among repulsive bedfellows.

There have been attempts by man to defame the holy word of God in the watering down to the low nature of man. These faith waters measured is from the book of Ezekiel is the full look at life. Ezekiel gets the first view as to understanding associated with the measuring of these waters. These waters that pre-dates time is of and in time. However, man has become more and more religious in self righteousness opposed to God's spiritual righteousness of "the truth that makes us free" (KJV John 8:32). Man has designed, in his mind, a heaven for himself and a hideous hell for others. Throughout religion is filled with dilemmas causing paradoxes that echoes from man's self-indulgent. Can we hear the pity-pat of itchy-bitchy little feet of the so-called giants of bedfellows trampling the clothed earth of God? As the prices continue to go up, there is something that we need to bear in mind as to the rest of that we write:

> Conservative columnist Thomas Sowell, an avid supporter of the Rothschild/Limbaugh /Reagan Bush/Cheney/Rockefeller Free Trade agenda, joined in this historically corrupt quest for ecomonics pick-pocketing, writing on December 17, 2008, which "creative destruction"—a good thing, he insists—means that American automakers and other manufacturers will just have to die and be replaced, having "outlived their usefulness"[10]

---

[10] Marrs, Texe. *America Being Torn Down and Rebuilt.* 2012.
http://www.texemarrs.com/022010/rothschilds_plan.htm (accessed January 8, 2013).

Many and most of the originators of a religious sect are extreme and bizarre. For example: There are those that believe when they die they get their own planet and become a god. These are in business of religion just for the money. There are many weirdos, which are still practicing weird religions; as well as, there are many weird so-called Christian. Somebody has to be wrong with there being over eight thousand (8000) different dominations in Christianity. It is here we must, "Let the Tares and Wheat grow together until the harvest" (KJV Matt. 13:30). These paradoxical (contradictory) religions jockeys for control over humanity wanting to be gods and lords of the entire world. These can range from the pundit to the pontiff. These individuals rarely sleep who give to us headaches with millions of aftershocks. These are they of the depraved and the wretched coldness who sit in their self made high places claiming supremacy.

The question of "How Long" has been before in the suffering. The understanding of the answer is one of ambiguity: "Until time be no more!" It is the tares planted into religions that have fleeced and flattered with an application rejecting some and accepting others. "Come unto me, all ye that labor and are heavy laden and I will give you rest" (KJV, Matt 11:28). There is the confidence that we can rest comfortably within the understanding of that "in all these things we are more than conquerors through him that loved us"(KJV Rom 8:37). This is a different kind of echo, which eradicates the hyperboles of man and allows God's word to flourish unadulterated. It is the self-indulged echo of religion, which modifies God's word. "I rebuke you" is the power of God's word where monsters no longer apprehend and lurk in the dark during further harm. The tares mixed with wheat causes these waters, in which we wrestle, to rise to extreme heights. The poisonous venom from the tares of Satan, through someone transforming himself into an angel of light; deceives the many. And so says the scripture, "And marvel not, for Satan, himself is transformed into an angel of light" (KJV 2 Cor 11:14).

Humanity has not a friend, listening to the echoes of self-indulgent religions, which speaks dishonesty without authority. The sowing of sinful seeds among bedfellows is not beguiling. Humanity suffers in these rising waters of mixed evil with good. Here man parade with a charade— misusing God's word pounces and prances like a bobble-headed doll—dances for greed in the selfish use for his own benefit. It is here gods, of these echoes in self-indulgent, is but a tools for personal gain planting tares disguised as wheat deepen these waters. The struggle and the wrestling are the troubles that we all endure on this side of the river.

Man is nearing an absolute conclusion. He has never been able to represent himself nor others because he is pulled asunder by many contrary winds of doctrine. These beat the waters (word) create many storms. God allows man to self-indulge himself with his claim alignment with God where exaggerations are satisfied with religious lust of lordship. As we know, "The flesh lusteth against the Spirit, and the Spirit against the flesh: and these are contrary the one to the other: so that ye cannot do the things that ye would" (KJV Gal 5:17). This can be from a vote in congress unto a vote in a congregation. How often are we caught up in the dish of lust being served to us cold? God's business and humanity business are put on hold to satisfy **"the my-way-religion."**

The travel to come is of God's word from the altar within God spewed out becomes a river encompassing all life. It is here we can only be charged with being a friend of humanity [*Amicus Humane Generis Lat.*] As scripture says, "Ointment and perfume rejoice the heart: so doth the sweetness of a man's friend by hearty counsel" (KJV Prov 27:9). This text speaks volume about God as "amicus humani generis: A friend of the human race."[11]

---

[11]inrebus.com. *Latin quotes, mottos and words of wisdom.* 2007.
http://www.inrebus.com/latinphrases_a.php (accessed January 8, 2013).

God's theocratic word and way—in spite of the many gods and priests—have an irreversible flow reaching the to and fro into the eternal destiny of man's end-times, back to God. The unadulterated word of God in the hearing creates dauntless spirits, which grows in the way of truth (Wheat) and not the others (tares). Leaning forward with hyperboles, it will be the "others (tares)" that will engulf and graft the pleasure-seeking of the self-indulgent. This is the general thinking of so many in these last days. As Stephen (2006) from his writing *Without Gods: toward a History of Disbelief* stated, "I think both religious and secular philosophies offer a variety of viewpoints as to how we are supposed to enjoy ourselves, the relative merits of physical vs. Mental/spiritual pleasures, and why such enjoyment constitutes a moral good."[12]

God abhor self-indulgent and did not create religions; but, rather, God has given flowing water (the word) for man to eat there from and live. In many instances, other voices have come alive today, as it was in the past such as, Fredrick Nietzsche, who spoke volumely asking the question:

---

[12] Stevens, Mitchell. *Without gods: toward a history of disbelief.* October 18, 2006.

http://www.futureofthebook.org/mitchellstephens/archives/2006/10/pleasure_v_reli.html (accessed January 9, 2013).

Have you not heard of that madman who lit a lantern in the bright, morning hours, ran to the marketplace, and cried incessantly: "I am looking for God! I am looking for God!" Goes on to say, "Thus spoke the devil to me once: God to have his hell: that is his love of man." And most recently I heard him say this: "God is dead; God died of his pity for man (Dictionary.com 2013).[13]

All things—be it politics, academia, or religions— need a premise. This premise or foundation is the spiritual underpinning, which is before the created flowings of life. Let it be further noted with an understanding that all flows are of the living. These flows of the word allowed a mixture of tares and wheat in this: a different kind of book. From the text [Ezekiel 47: 1-7], in the context mindful of pretext, and post-text erects and arrests the attention of everything and everyone. God's word is never ancient as was in ancient times in the not knowing the location of Job's land of Uz to which scripture asks, "Shall any teach God knowledge? Seeing he judgeth those that are high"(KJV Job 21:22). Here and there in the opens of life; it is the foretelling from the book of Ezekiel 47 that writes the rest of the story.

---

[13] Dictionary.com. "God is Dead." Dictionary of Quotes. 2013. http://quotes.dictionary.com/search/god_is_dead (accessed March 9, 2013).

GOD

"Afterward he brought me again..." (KJV, Ezekiel 47:1)

God, for all intents and purposes, is an infinite spirit who created and rules the universe and is the source of all moral authority. God moved Ezekiel from one dispensation to another as to the conceptualization of the word *"again."* God the "Omni of everything" gives "the-all" to Ezekiel. God, as with everything, transcends is unlimited. According to Ewin Hubble (n.d), "About 15 billion years ago a tremendous explosion started the expansion of the universe. This explosion is known as the Big Bang (LaRocco and Rothstein n. d.).[14] This is the admittance of Science. God can be a science in the sense of "Omniscience." Omniscience relative to the science of man places God beyond the Big Bang by the state that the Big Bang was only an expansion; whereas, God is the creator before the bang and the expansion. As a thesis, all we can say, "God was before there was a was--and was the "was" of the before, which is the is of is--will forever be with all power, 'Omnipotent.'"

---

[14] LaRocco, Chris, and Blair Rothstein. *The Big Bang*. n. d. http://www.umich.edu/~gs265/bigbang.htm (accessed January 27, 2013).

Science and Theology get a shock as to the inseparability of God and science. There was an old preacher who was asked about the big bang who stated, "The big bang that man talks about is no more than the fart coming out of the rear-end of God relative to all the workings of God." Scientists, as in the big bang, will be searching until life is no more trying to get to the origin of the scent. Their noses will become intoxicated to death before sniffing an origin. Deputy Dog out on a fishing expedition. The resolution is "God" of the text—the beginning and the end—yet, elusive to science because there is no other beside God. "And Jacob awaked out of his sleep, and he said, Surely the LORD is in this place; and I knew it not. And he was afraid, and said, How dreadful is this place! This is none other but the house of God, and this is the gate of heaven" (KJV, Ge 28:16-17.

Life's revelation reveals, as we wrestle in deep waters, tares and wheat are both under and in the control of God. This is so, even, when it does not seem so. Yet, because of our free will agency we are left without the spirit controlling—if we are not saved—*Wrestling In Deep Waters* is pronounced the more. Ezekiel: "*Afterward he brought me again. . .*" is an acknowledged affirmation of no privilege; it is to "the we know not where." Was it as to all the worlds, planets, stars, wind and air, light and darkness, houses and lands, and infinity, which is/was all one and in/was/is one as to God being inseparable? "And he [God] is before all things, and by him all things consist" (KJV, Colossians 1:17).

It is here—within the text—God has made a separation for the convenience of everything. According to Wesley (n.d), "The original expression not only implies that he sustains all things in being, but more directly, all things were and are compacted in him into one system. He is the cement, as well as support, of the universe" (Biblos 2011).[15] Another way of looking at thing is for one to say that God decided to make for himself some toys and some creatures.

God the creator, made even the Devil, as one of his toys. This is not nitpicking; this is just the reasonable excerpt that Satan was created by God. Satan knew all of God's word and God's heart in his design for all of this world. It was in the heart of God that everything was absolutely beautiful, and this is why Satan wanted to be God. According to Litke (1975) surveying the bible states "Satan is the Devil (slanderer), Lucifer (son of the morning), Beelzebub (Lord of the flies – Matt.12:24), and Belial (lawless – 2 Cor. 6:15), the evil one (1 John 5:19),

---

[15] Biblos. *Bible Suite by Biblos: Westley Notes*. 2011. http://bible.cc/colossians/1-17.htm (accessed 1 25, 2013).

the tempter (1 Thess.3:5), the prince of this world (John 12:31), the god of this age (2 Cor.4:4), the prince of the power of the air (Eph.2:2), the accuser of the brethren (Rev.12:10), and angel of light (false light – 2 Cor.11:14), a serpent (Rev.12:9), and a dragon (Rev.12:3).[16]

Reading any verse or clinging to any one word from the book of Ezekiel, the beginning and ending production is: there is none other than God. The allegories of God are extended to us for growth and profit and, yet, have become a paradox. God flowing —through the reading out of Ezekiel—pitched a completed three sixty circle of life back to himself without ever lifting a finger. God has not wrapped anyone around the axle wheel of existence in a loop of no resolve; and, yet, the circumstance will never change because God said it: "For I am the LORD, I change not..." (KJV, Mal 3:6).

Hermeneutically, the discourse is to whatever exists changes not who God is. However, man's hermeneutics are his discourse to a sermon using some science or methodology concerned with explaining or interpreting religious concepts, theories, and principles

---

[16] Biblos. *Bible Suite by Biblos: Westley Notes.* 2011. http://bible.cc/colossians/1-17.htm (accessed 1 25, 2013).

relating to a text. Away from such and back to the topic, "God is just God!" There, as to what else in the absolute, knows we of raised hands, shrugged shoulders, bowed knees, and with lips of no choice but to praise God. God never disappoints us as to his personhood. With recognition, it is God himself who speaks saying, "Before I formed thee in the belly I knew thee; and before thou camest forth out of the womb I sanctified thee, and I ordained thee a prophet unto the nations" (KJV Jer 1:5).

God is the specifics revealed after centuries of the experienced. With life far spent, there is only the knowing in part by us; whereas, God knows the "missing part" that we are not aware of as we exist. It is this in-part-ness that scripture says, "For I would not, brethren, that ye should be ignorant of this mystery, lest ye should be wise in your own conceits; that blindness in part is happened to Israel, until the fulness of the Gentiles be come in" (KJV Rom 11:25).

God of the text of Ezekiel point to the fact that "GOD" is the beginning or starting point all waters because the water was "before" the house. This water referenced in Ezekiel 47 is God's word. The water is of God, the water is the word, God is his word; similarly, God's word is one in the same with the water and is also God; so is: "the house," "the door," and "the altar." Awesome, isn't it? The more we know it seems the less our abilities. . ... Ezekiel, for the most part, did virtually nothing. God took Ezekiel, and Ezekiel had nothing that he could say about the taking. This should humble all of us! It is here to say "in the not so distant" a transitional input is without questioning. With attention to—"in the not so distant"—the metaphors, here, are so entrenched shake our inabilities within the milieu of our finiteness accept God as infinite of the absolute. This is why John recanted himself in the denouncing of his restricted ability and just said,

> In the beginning was the Word, and the Word was with God, and the Word was God. The same was in the beginning with God. All things were made by him; and without him was not any thing made that was made. In him was life; and the life was the light of men. And the light shineth in darkness; and the darkness comprehended it not (KJV John 1:1-5).

In the constant search and unearthing, the termination circles to the one God: everything by himself, and all else exist from/because of this one God. There are breakdown juxtapositions for our convenience—often not understood—to give us a glimpse of perfection. To some degree, we can decipher the simplicity of non simple—simple. The learned position is that, if were simple, that is good enough. In this case, this is why the Psalmist said, "The entrance of thy words giveth light; it giveth understanding unto the simple" (KJV, Ps 119:130).

It is most difficult for the mind of a purely academician being to comprehend the God of no beginning and no end. Not being naïve! It is here where many systems of the world's best scholars are in the non-acceptance of this very fact that there a God. However, everyone and everything knows that there is something, whether or not scientists will admit such or not. Even today, these same scientists, with and through his mighty inventions, are constantly looking up for a discovery. Man is looking up to prove their theories, but their proofs prove the point of God's existence as a man looks up and sees the multiple galaxies of no end. Then, he tells himself that there, here, is no factuality. In return, God is dismissed in the reverse order of things as the built instruments get the glory.

When expressed as fact, God becomes a "stand alone" as a myth; in other words, scientists and scholars (over intellectuals) will never accept a scientific myth as a stand alone. They would rather plant "*Tares*" in the "*Wheat*" and create paradoxes. Therefore, the belief in, on or about God as an accepted concept is not admitted to beyond the Big Bang in direct wordings. God is not admitted too, as a fact expressed, in the circumlocutory describing the Big Band expansion of the universe. Well, would you not say, "If there was/is a Big Bang, there has to be a 'BANGER?'" For every "bang" that I have known throughout my lifetime, there has been someone or something behind the bang [every time I write bang, my computer want me use "barn" "LOL"] doing the banging, once more tares and wheat. Who says that Christians do not have a sense of humor?

Furthering the humor and for hilarity sakes, it has been said, "God directs the **Bang** and the **Buck**. This is an imaginary concert of understanding in living as to God's no-end-infinite-attributes." Afterwardly, try immutability—"For I am the LORD, I change not..." (KJV, Mal 3:6). The supercomputers of comparisons and observations as a new control norm have attempted to replace God. This God that "brought Ezekiel again..." (Ez. 47:1) is a God of transcendency. He is the "beyond of when or where!" God carried Ezekiel beyond the designed supercomputer to God's matrix: "**Worlds** without end." God is just God and all we can say, "Through faith we understand that the **"worlds"** were framed by the word of God, so that things which are seen were not made of things which do appear" (KJV Heb 11:3). Normally, this would be out of an alignment of the rational, but these new conditional norms are no longer the boundary limits. The bang/buck starts and returns to the origin and guess who composed the universe as the capsulized infinity of beginning—God! Scripture will suffice and bring to a climax with the saying, "Hath in these last days spoken unto us by his Son, whom he hath appointed heir of all things, by whom also he made the **'worlds'"**(KJV, Heb 1:2).

God is the grid of stability. It is the going outside of God's grid that creates all instability. This is how tares get mixed with wheat: leaving the grid. Man, as snake in the grass, speaks a poisoned, venomous word that mixes with God's word that tears and rips at our foundation causing a mighty "wrestling." All was; all is; and all to be is where all have always been—in the **MIND of GOD**, which is the grid of God. If man could destroy the least atom, he could and would destroy God. As for such, the closest man has come to the destroying himself and God is the splitting of an atom [making of an atomic bomb]. If Hubble can "bang" in a theory; then, it is only reasonable that another can do the same, right? The "Mind of God" theory sound good, doesn't it? It is only the unrealistic associated with religious experiences is how hyperboles open the theoretical for lunatics. Yet, it cannot be answered how God carries one *"again. . ."* talking about Ezekiel as we *Wrestle In Deep Waters*. The grid of God is near, yet so far, and all sights are dim. "For now we see through a glass, darkly; but then face to face: now I know in part; but then shall I know even as also I am known" (KJV 1 Cor 13:12).

As we continue to look through a glass, darkly... God responds to us saying, "For my thoughts are not your thought, neither are your ways my ways. For as the heavens are higher than the earth, so are my ways higher than your ways, and my thoughts than your thoughts" (KJV, Isa 55:8-9). The galaxies are far-reaching in the beyond of no end. God with no missed iota simultaneously and instantaneously— with perfection and no error—synchronized his infinity in the manipulation of worlds with time to spare, toyed with the follies and likes of humans. Not only humans: picture and grasp the dimensions of an elephant and the dimensions of a gnat, the gnat with God gets equal care as does the elephant. He gives no less to the gnat and no more to the elephant than does he to the gnat. Here and consequently, "God is a Spirit: and they that worship him must worship him in spirit and in truth" (KJV John 4:24). Meaning "God: this Spirit" is everything—around and within the infinitesimal atom—it is all God.

Just as God with no ending and beginning, it is here also in this writing—and this pondering upon and in the spirit of the spirit—there is no ending as to this augury preoccupation with the infinite. The growth is always the swelling words, some "tares" and some "wheat" but none can undo the done as to nullifying God and the abolishing of existence. This is not argumentation; however, if so, as a philosophical thought comprising a question, "Would this too, as to everything and everywhere of non existence, be also with God still in and an existence?" God is not a dinosaur remnant left for cosmological archaeologists to dust and sift in some moon's sand to say now this is God. Yet God's Omni[s] are etched to an in everything imaginable. Not only the moon and stars above, but, here of the worlds seen and unseen, which are without end as God himself is infinite without ending.

God is a spirit in the sense of whatever is; IS! Whenever is; IS! Wherever is; IS! There is; IS! Ever is; IS! If not is, IS—or, will be-ever is, IS! God, from the best mind attempting an explanation of "Him" being "Him" does not scratch the surface as to the "Who"—Who of GOD? There is such a thing as madness to a no conclusion relating to God. And the scripture says, "And they were filled with madness; and communed one with another they might do to Jesus" (KJV Luke 6:11). The presumed deduction of logic within any one particular as a reasoned assumption attempts to frame God to an intelligent cause as a means is too an illogical deduction that furthers man's finiteness and God's infiniteness.

It is God in the support of being God, which binds the every as to himself!" God created the universe; "God created God! If, you disagree; then, prove God existence without God creating God. This presumption beyond the state just takes us to more madness. However and whatever! If as the atheist believes, there is no God. Then, what proves the origin "OF?" Who, what, or how can there ever be a conclusion to anything?

As to the beginning origin, what would one call it, other than God? If all were of a bang (big or little), who or what caused "thee" of the banged or the banging. The logic and evidence of every great mind looking into the mind of God's existence begins with the who. God is just simply God; or otherwise, all is full of "Holy Holes." Only the infinite can explain infinite and finite the vise-versa. God explains God and explains all others. The all others are only God's byproducts [spin-off] that return to the product [creator] —God. God is just God. As simply stated, these simple small seemingly words are the very point of being God. Any other is *Wrestling In Deep Waters*. The point of the "OF" does not shrink the immeasurable; but rather, with tares and wheat, there is given a profound growth. All is in as to bringing everything back to God as a belonging! "And not holding the Head, from which all the body by joints and bands having nourishment ministered, and knit together, increaseth with the increase of God" (KJV Col. 2:19.

Most readers have not heard of the word "Pantheism." It is a philosophy that sees God as/in everything; and, yet, God transcends and/is beyond the everything. The doctrine that God is the transcendent reality of which the material universe and human experiences are only manifestations manifested from various religious belief or philosophical doctrine that identifies God with the universe.[17] God is God and no more! Whereas, the certainty of scripture reveals a reality, which comes to life as to these words, "And to make all men see what is the fellowship of the mystery which from the beginning of the world hath been hid in God, who created all things by Jesus Christ"(KJV Eph 3:9).

So what is this beginning conclusion that will never conclude: God created everything from the word; and, if, there was no word (which is God), there would be no universe [world/worlds], no Ezekiel, nor you, or me. The writing is easy as to the given, but the unambiguous knowing is an eluding dance, which skip a beat in the mind. We are taken, as it was with Ezekiel, as God did the bringing him again to help us understand Paul's stated: "For now we see through a glass, darkly; but then face to face: now I know in part; but then shall I know even as also I am known" (KJV 1 Cor 13:12).

---

[17] Dictionary.com. "pantheism." *Dictionary.com*. 2013.
http://dictionary.reference.com/browse/pantheism?s=t (accessed February 2, 2013).

"Afterward he brought me again..." (KJV, Ezekiel 47:1, [l. 1]).

Ezekiel

Afterward he brought me again... (KJV, Ezekiel 47:1,

[L. 1])

Ezekiel is a prophet during the Israelites early years of captivity. His literary works are full of rhetorical metaphors associated with many inclusions. In chapter 47, Ezekiel metaphors are all inclusive as we look at water and the measuring thereof of these waters depicting God prophetic perspective on how his word mixed with the words of man has grown these waters. According to Campbell and Huxman (2009), "A 'perspective,' literally, is a way of looking through (*per* = through; *specere* = to look), an angle of vision, a way of seeing" (p. 1).[18] This is in no way to nullify the power of God in the working through the experiences of Ezekiel. This is just the backdrop as to the pedigree of the man Ezekiel, and his associated lineage. It is mostly of conjecture as to how Ezekiel gets much of his acclaim; nonetheless, his fame is renown as "God's Man," with us, using a play on words.

---

[18] Huxman, Karlyn Kohrs Campbell and Susan Schultz. *The Rhetorical Act: Thinking, Speaking, and Writing Critically.* Belmont,CA: Wadsworth Cengage Learning, 2009.

Supposition spins us to seeing Ezekiel— more likely than not—as being a member of the Zadok clan. This is not planting tares in the wheat field; quite frankly, this is just the best information that we can gather as to the personhood of Ezekiel, other than being a priest. Nonetheless, it seems from scripture that Ezekiel rose to prominence was not from the fact that he was a priest in Jerusalem; rather from, his call to prophesy in 593 B. C. It should be of interest, under strict notation, that Ezekiel had a bitter indifference against his own people because they had become hedonistic (self-indulged, pleasure seekers) contrary to priestly teaching.

Ezekiel—in the portrayal of his works, as a prophet—arranged his works "systematically in four divisions, chapter 1–24, chapter 25–32, chapter 33–39, and chapter 40–48"(p. 14).[19] As to conjecture, Ezekiel's work is systematically arranged because of the quality of work that the scribes were doing in their hayday. Exact dates occurs 13 times detailing that Ezekiel received prophecies from God relating to the circumstances in the children of God lives as to their captivity.

It is here, somewhere around 593 B.C., in Ezekiel's fifth year of captivity where God comprehensively uses

<hr />

[19]Encyclopedia Britannica, Inc. *Encyclopedia Britannica*. Chicago: London: Toronto: William Benton, 1960.

Ezekiel. Ezekiel was given God's prophetic playbook, which open past, present and future association with creation's work and God's word growing. It is "the-could-of" that make most men jealous to the going mad for jealousy. God has made us in his image and after his likeness and the scriptures say, "For the LORD, whose name is Jealous, is a jealous God" (KJV Ex 34:14) gives us no right to this same jealousy. So here, it was not you; it was Ezekiel that was brought to this place. The "me" underscored here in Ezekiel 47:1 line 1 is the prophet Ezekiel.

Although, it could have been just as well as you; however, it was not. It was Ezekiel! According to the Jewish bible, "Ezekiel was the son of Buzi, the priest, in the land of the Chaldeans, by the river Chebar and exiled to the mighty Babylonian empire under the kingship of Nebuchadnezzar" (Yechezkel –Ezekiel – Ch 1. v. 3).[20] Ezekiel was a devout prophet despite his circumstances. The transiency flight of Ezekiel as God takes him to the beginning understandable essence of man for a glimpse at how "it all" was released. It is here in the possiblity knowledge that God lets Ezekiel know a hair more than us, because, we

---

[20] Chabad-Lubavitch Media Center. "Yechezkel - Ezekiel - Chapter 1 verse 3." *The Jewish Complete Bible.* 2013.
http://www.chabad.org/library/bible_cdo/aid/16099/jewish/Chapter-1.htm#v1 (accessed February 13, 2013).

know nothing.   Sanity keep us from attempting to reach to far beyond the most part of now.   We wrestle; but for the crazies, their wrestle is uncertain.

The corroborative illumination from research of history and scripture paints an arduous portrait of Ezekiel, which is by far unmatched.   The closest that I was able to find was the accounts of Daniel and the three Hebrew Boys—"Shadrach, Meshach, and Abednego, in the province of Babylon." (KJV Dan 3:30). Ezekiel like Daniel was God's prophet.   Ezekiel was not only a prophet; Ezekiel was a great teacher who taught the revival of a nation which gives us our present day Isreal.   Yet, most of us knows Ezekiel best associated with the "Valley of Dry Bones" (Ezekiel 37). God's revelation to Ezekiel for Isreal increased and flourished as dressed bones came together with covered skin connected an old, old valley demonstrating the growing power of God's word without the infections.   The Jewish people have a state and homeland that fulfilled God's promise.

There are no prophets of history, which have gone where Ezekiel has gone as to the carrying of God. We can look at Moses seeing God's back parts, (Ex. 33:23) Enoch "Tranlation" (Heb 11:5), Jacob as to "Jacob's Ladder"(Gen. 28:12), Paul's "Third Heaven" (2 Cor. 12:2) or John out on the Isle called Patmos, New Heaven's vision (Rev. 21:1), but to be taken and showen everything, there are none like

Ezekiel here in this 47th Chapter. It is not the beginning of the word, but this is the beginning flowing of the word in the moving involvement with the life of man. It is true—we say many sweet, sounding, catchy phrases like: **"God can do anything but fail."** Naturally, this is absolutely true in "all-standings."

The imposition is of a question, "How can one see God's beginning when God has always been without a beginning? It is here at the same time that God knew the end before the beginning. For the pseudointellectual, this can be problematic. The pointedness of their knowledge can only reach to the **dead sea scrolls**. Then Solomon, with proverbial widsom, succumbed and spoke on this wise judiciously said, "The LORD possessed me in the beginning of his way, before his works of old. I was set up from everlasting, from the beginning, or before ever the earth was" (KJV, Prov 8:22-23).

As a fact, we know the earth was not where it is now because God had not spoken it into existence, yet, it existed. If this is to make any sense at all, we must accept the fact that—**"WAS"**—was before everlasting, which later became beginning by the word. "In the beginning was the Word, and the Word was with God, and the Word was God. The same was in the beginning with God. All things were made by him; and without him was not any thing made that was made" (KJV, John 1:1-3).

Ezekiel is unique because of the—"*afterward he brought me again. . .*"—after-fact of happenings. Ezekiel got to see it all from the inception of the "FLOW FROM" (Instant Replay before Replay). Yet, it had already happened, but as we will learn as we read on, Ezekiel saw more than what had happened. God jettisoned Ezekiel to the beyond to the even now—whether or not he understood what was going on or what was happening is a matter of conjecture. This is fascinating stuff, isn't it? Here is another point that is so amazing: The scene of future things, partipating in them, and not to be of them gets a recording for others, of future times, to introspect for understanding and guidance.

Ezekiel—maybe we have it— God was-was/is eternal is beginning was-was/is "word," and all is God to the wildest of imagination as far as mind's eye can see. Since, there was nothing but God scripture says, "Without him was not any thing made that was made" (KJV John 1:3). As a result, Ezekiel is getting no more than a glimpse of a pebble juxtaposed existence partially seeing waters rise. Have you ever looked down at a thing and in your mind you saw it—but it was not physical? "How is this," you may ask? This is how we grew; and all the while, we were growing (wide awake) only realized that we had grown when that dress or suit no longer fit. While growing, getting bigger, we recognized nothing, did we? This growing grew and came into existence before a physical reality of being as the living; yet, it lived. Imagine the conversation that Ezekiel was having with himself and God. The hip Ezekiel probably said, "Oh, thanks God! I see; this is so cool!"

Ezekiel was carried away from Jerusalem several years before the destruction of Jerusalem. Just the thought of the all-encompassing is so profound. Ezekiel out of the loins and lineage of priests now a prisoner in a foreign land is again and is now taken again to a place of God where God shows his will and his way. This is with Ezekiel as with all men in this place where God gives prophecies that present to man or men things to come. Far-out, to say to say the least.

Ezekiel, in the spirit, received a forward look that is the constant extension of God. In this vision, this is the knowing who Ezekiel was as to the knowing life within God and therefrom. Solomon in his widsom said, "The thing that hath been, it is that which shall be; and that which is done is that which shall be done: and there is no new thing under the sun" (KJV Eccl 1:9). Ezekiel—the worthy one—got what only a few men ever get; the chance to see prior to the recorded word biblically. There are no new prophesies, just prophesies that have been revealed through the written word after the writing.

Ezekiel, just so happened to be God's prophet of the moment for the moment. This is a humbling time because whatever in the thinking—the thinker is just in the moment for a moment. "In a moment, in a twinkling of eye. . ." (KJV, 1Cor 15:52). As to this moment there is an the old saying that says, "Men solve problems and get things done in-spite of the difficulties right now (this moment)." Captivity is not an easy chore. Captivity is not meant for no race of people, regardless of generation or century, or culture and is not of God. Slavery is slavery; whereas, one is at the mercy of the slaver. All slavers from time to time have been cruel and are not Godly. If you think to the contrary, you have a hole in your brains, not just your head.

Ezekiel being a man had a rougher time than most, but the real man part of Ezekiel was unlike the rest of the captured, carried way of his day. Ezekiel did not blame his forefathers. Just as most, we have no justification for embracing much of anything that our forefathers have done. With the children of Israel in captivity, this is to their complaining and blaming, which is called "Sour Grapes— 'the fathers eat the sour grapes, But the children's teeth are set on edge? As I live declare the Lord God, you are surely not going to use this proverb in Israel anymore'" (KJV, Ezekiel 18:1-3).

Ezekiel was a refreshing contrast to other so called prophets. It is like the present day of living among the "great pretenders." They live among us, and we live with and among them. This is how tares get mixed in with the wheat. This is why we are *Wrestling In Deep Waters*. We do not make direct "pointed finger" judgement as to any —for the most part in our minds—because when we think we know; we really don't know. This is why the scripture says, "For such are false apostles, deceitful workers, transforming themselves into the apostles of Christ. And no marvel; for Satan himself is transformed into an angel of light" (KJV 2 Cor 11:13-14). This is why the scripture goes on to further say:

> But he said, nay; lest while ye gather up the tares, ye root up also the wheat with them. Let both grow together until the harvest: and at the time of harvest I will say to the reapers, Gather ye together first the tares, and bind them in bundles to burn them: but gather the wheat into my barn (KJV Matt 13:29-30).

God has given us so many prophetic characters in the chronology of time. We know Jesus in his incarnated state. We know about the disciples and works following Jesus resurrection. We know about Abraham, Issac, and Jacob. This list goes on and on with inclusion of David, Solomon. Daniel, Job, and recently Dr. King. Ezekiel gets a role in life's cast that almost outshines all men accept the man Jesus and John the Baptist.

"Assuredly, I say to you, among those born of women there has not risen one greater than John the Baptist; but he who is least in the kingdom of heaven is greater than he" (KJV, Mt 11:11). As for the rest, we have to let the wheat and the tares grow together. Does this sound about right?

Ezekiel's first hand personal experiences (our today's everyday experiences) beforehand gives rise to God's favor. This is what foresight is all about. It is what's called "born with a veil" over one's face." A distant view to a place and time of certainties that one knows but cannot do much about other than warn. The people have to make the right choice for a heavenly placement escaping hell's fire. It is here with Ezekiel that even Matthew Henry reaches to understand and agree with the spirit when he says two every important thing about the 47th chapter of Ezekiel:

I. The vision of the holy waters, their rise, extent, depth, and healing virtue, the plenty of fish in them, and an account of the trees growing on the banks of them (v. 1-12).

II. An appointment of the borders of the land of Canaan, which was to be divided by lot to the tribes of Israel and the strangers that sojourned among them (v. 13-23).[21]

Ezekiel's writing as to the stated confounds the mind to this very moment about the *"Afterward he **brought me again. . ."** (KJV, Ezekiel 47:1, [L. 1])*. For years, I had studied commentary after commentary, and it wasn't until this very second the darning took place. This "**brought me again. . .**" to what a trip that slipped my understanding is as of the forty six (46) chapters before this 47th chapter of Ezekiel. Now I have it! God did give Ezekiel forty six (46) others prior to taken Ezekiel to the place to get this new 47th chapter's peep. Then ushered Ezekiel back again and projected him into the future of the word. Thus, this word of Ezekiel that is applied to us is for this day, and in this moment of time for our unique set of circumstances. Ezekiel's constancy in the coming back again with the carrying of God shows us that *Wrestling In Deep Waters* is a continuous ongoing affair in life of the living. God did not end at the 47th chapter— but for good measure; Ezekiel received a 48th invitation.

---

[21] BibleStudyTools. "Mathew Henry Comentary Ezekiel 47." Bible Study Tools.com: growing deep into the word. 2013.
http://www.biblestudytools.com/commentaries/matthew-henry-complete/ezekiel/47.html (accessed February 15, 2013).

Ezekiel comes to us with the children of Isreal in captivity with Ezekiel having a vision. The scripture says, "Now it came to pass in the thirtieth year, in the fourth month, on the fifth day of the month, as I was among the captives by the River Chebar, that the heavens were opened and I saw visions" (KJV, Eze 1:1). It is in this vision of Ezekiel that he sees some strange things: "Four creature with four heads and these heads look like people and animals with animals and fowls parts." (KJV, Eze 1: 2-4). Then, all of a sudden in chapter 2 Ezekiel is called to be a prophet. It is here Ezekiel reports that God says:

> Son of man, I am sending you to the children of Israel, to a rebellious nation that has rebelled against Me; they and their fathers have transgressed against Me to this very day. 4 For they are impudent and stubborn children. I am sending you to them, and you shall say to them, 'Thus says the Lord GOD.' 5 As for them, whether they hear or whether they refuse — for they are a rebellious house — yet they will know that a prophet has been among them (KJV Eze 2:3-5).

We see not Ezekiel attempting to refuse God in any way, fashion, or form, as so many reject God today in service. As we all know, this was not the case with Jonah. Jonah ran! Some called him a coward, and another says that most ran from the call of God. How many of us wish to be responsible, but as God know us, we are a group of impudent and stubborn people. This word, "impudent," that Ezekiel uses is what God called the children of Isreal. Impudent is a word meaning "rude" as to showing a lack of respect and excessive boldness after not showing respect. We all have had the experience with the bully in school, on the playground, or even, in your family that needs a good size bibical lick upside the head because of his or her attitude. The folks that God are now telling Ezekiel to lead are ill-mannered, disrespectful, and just flat out savages.

Ezekiel gets his importance as a major prophet in his time of struggle during captivity. This is important because major prophets of God were not just privileged to the visionary affairs of their days. These major prophets—the like of Ezekiel—were privileged to long sighted reach into the future that includes our present day circumstances and involvements with service and worship. Ezekiel is a prophet— called of God!

[u]nto the door… (KJV, Ezekiel 47:1, [L. 1])

DOOR

"[U]nto the door..." (KJV, Ezekiel 47: 1, [L. 1])

"And he brought me into the inner court of the LORD's house, and, behold, at the door of the temple of the LORD, between the porch and the altar, were about five and twenty men, with their backs toward the temple of the LORD, and their face toward the east; and they worshipped the sun toward the east" (KJV, Eze. 8:16). In the vicinity of an area adjacent to a location of God's Vision, to Ezekiel, all reverence God with trembling and fear. Let's finish painting the picture: see all the weird creatures. These have heads that look like men, and they have legs like that of a lion (cat) with the feet of eagle's claws, and they do fly. Imagine, suddenly here, and a voice calls your name, "Ezekiel!" "Ezekiel!" As a door opens, would you be trembling?

"Unto the door. . ." (Ez. 47:1). The scripture says, "Serve the LORD with fear, and rejoice with trembling" (KJV, Ps 2:11-12). "Then said Jesus unto them again, Verily, verily, I say unto you, I am the door of the sheep" (KJV John 10:7). Referring to the "tares" these are vented words purporting to be the word of God. This painted picture and these goings on, here at the door and in the arms of God, Ezekiel probably is not too comely. His spirit is mixed with excitement or reverence and fear. Ezekiel receives the true understanding of what these *tares* are implanted among the *wheat*. God lets without approval as to growth of the unintended paradox.

[*Before a topic sentence to start this paragraph, here is a bit of offbeat humor: some years ago living at home with my parents, I pretend to be angry. It's here I said to my mother, "This is the reason I'll be leaving here." My mother grabbed the dinner plate out of my hand and said to me, 'On your way out don't let the door knob hit you where the Lord split you.'"* **Don't forget that doors have doorknobs!** *"LOL"*]

While living, there is the forgetting many things along the way on life's journey. Therefore, God in his own way remind us of the forgotten. This is when it seems as if history is repeating itself as things of our past adventures resurface to reinforce realism. Admittedly, it might take a couple of kicks in the **"you-know-what,"** and there is that itch that has to be scratched, right? Within religion, there is the need for continued reinforcements. It is here even with Ezekiel "brought again to the door of the house. . ." (KJV, Ezekiel. 41:1) that the scripture's context points to an omnipotent God—over and over again—working on and in us after taking us to a place of the primary. This is the attempted determination. As to the origin of religion, it can be said:

There are two broad groups of theories about the origin of religion, which are the Faith-based theories typically based on revelation from one or more deities—mainly gods and goddesses, and the secular based theories where anthropologists, evolutionary biologists, and other researchers have reached a near consensus that humans of the species homo sapiens evolved from a species of proto-humans who originated somewhere in Africa. This gave proto-humans an improved ability to pass on their accumulated knowledge to their descendents, to form more advanced societies, and ultimately to create religions.[22]

What is it that can be considered trustworhy? Words are power and powerful. Liking to the appeal of any one word remaining credible, the word itself must furnish both the genre and differentia of itself. This is why religion gets to be complicated with many different word meaning. It is within religion the inner none trust that trouble the being and ultimately causes wars that kills and maims. Ezekiel speaks of "the door" (47:1). Words etymology begin the process of grouping and lumping sentence meaning together. In the thereafter, there has to be distinguished in the differentia of the same spelled word a different understanding relating to connotations & denotations.

[22] Robinson, B. A. *Some theories on the origin of religion*. March 15, 2009. http://www.religioustolerance.org/rel_theory1.htm (accessed January 10, 2013).

These understandings associated with words are very important. The satisfactions are not just the Echoes of the Self-Indulged Religions.

The word of power, once the filling up thereof, begins to move between words strikes fear. It is in this we wrestle with that we cannot trust. Many instances it the hearing of many echoes that furthers our *Wrestling In Deep Waters*. The door unlocks after a completed filling to never lock again, yet, another echo come. It was at Boston University, Marsh Chapel that Dr. Thurman (1971) "[r]esounded in the knowledge of "in the searching restlessness for which the word's 'spirit' seems more appropriate, the life inherited is always moving toward goals and ends that are sensed only when realized" (Howard Thurman PhD, 1971, p. 14).[23] All here is metaphoric; at the same time, the literal is only emblematical as from the door contrast at Marsh Chapel—but the echoes continue to "resound."

There is much to be taken into consideration as we discuss the door. It is here where Ezekiel had been before, and it is a place where most of us have been before without realizing it. Before delving deep into

---

[23] PhD., Howard Thurman. The Inward Journey. 9 vols. Richmond, IN: Friends United Press, 1971

what is meant by the forgone statement just made, let us look at couple of biblical scriptures to help broaden our understanding of the text. "And God said, Let us make man in our image, after our likeness" (KJV Gen 1:26). Secondly, 1 Cor 6:19 states, "Know ye not that your body is the temple of the Holy Ghost which is in you" (KJV). God replicates his bigness image and likeness; then, God miniaturized this image and likeness down to us being what is now called living creatures.

The journeying to the door with strength of character will persistently transport us back to God **"the whole of everything."** For the discernment of anything, it is this "door" that opens allowing sight as to the knowing and the receiving of anything. The tales completeness is of God's will in the sense that we are nothing apart from his being. Walking and breathing like all mortal, the travel for any, at any time needs a spirit's connection. This is not framing the experience of Ezekiel or the experience of others. The word expressly defined this "door" where now Ezekiel is standing in the presence of God—and, once more, "Then said Jesus unto them again, Verily, verily, I say unto you, I am the door of the sheep" (KJV John 10:7). The "door" is not a proposition to be sold; on the other hand, this is the entrance into life with benefits. With strenght of charater, we revert back to God's blessings.

While doing research as to the material in this book, humorously, life insurance as a human instrument is halarious. Think about it! Life insurance is only good, for the most part, after you are dead. In contrast, I did excerpt this quote for Lincoln Life, which stated: "Fixed life insurance includes a second-to-die life insurance product" (Allstate, 2013).[24] I had to abandon this "third person" writing and turn to the now the first person. The reason being is "life" is personal. The other day a fellow was asked a question, "If your dog is barking at the back door and your wife is yelling at the front door, who do you let in first?" The fellow answered, "The Dog of course—at least the dog will shut up after you let him in!" LOL!!! It is here both life and death is knocking at the door. Which one will you let in?

The door to life is a transcendency of everything past, present and future. Lincoln Life may be a great product as to future's death but fails the test as to future living. With all the good it does and has done, the "transcending door" has the more benefits because it does not speak of death in the sense of dying. Accordingly, the scriptures state:

---

[24] Allstate. (2013). *Lincoln Benefit Life Company Info.* Retrieved February 16, 2013, from Allstate:
https://www.accessallstate.com/anon/companyinfolbll.aspx

Jesus said unto her, I am the resurrection, and the life: he that believeth in me, though he was dead, yet shall he live: And whosoever liveth and believeth in me shall never die. Believest thou this" (KJV John 11:25-26)?

"Unto the door," the meaning is the coming into eternal life where there is no more death, but you must come to the "door." Ezekiel was "brought again unto the door" *(KJV, Ezekiel 47:1)*.

"[t]he door of the house ..." (KJV, Ezekiel 47:1 [l. 1])

House

"[T]he door of the house. . ." (KJV, Ezekiel 47:1 [l. 1])

Benjamin Franklin said, "A house is not a home unless it contained food and fire for the mind as well for the body." It is here of "resting and security," which connote and suggest to us our pictorial image of what a house should represent. In the same context there is the suggestion that if it is our house there are marvelously and heavenly associates that dwells in us. Allow me to take you over to the muddy part of the river as we continue *Wrestling In Deep Waters.*

For argument's sake using a few questions: Would there be a continual listening audience if the broadcast Sunday after Sunday stated heaven's road is dirty, the streets are cracked with the gold, missing? Would there be a winning appeal to make heaven your heavenly home? If heaven's walls were made of glass instead of jasper, would we still want to go to heaven? The road is dirty; the river is muddy; nine months out of the year weeds are choking the life out of all of the edibles; and the weather is cold the year round, would you still want to go to heaven? Bear in mind that heaven is the House of God. A young lady of the night overheard this series of questions and stated: "If God could not do any better than that; I am going to stick with the Devil." LOL!!!

God's house is called heaven. In the eschatology of Christianity, many believe this house of Ezekiel narrative is the place where the servants of God rest. Despite your queries, can we envisage God's Heaven as the house of God? Even to the thief on the cross, Jesus speaks of heaven and his home and said to the thief, "And Jesus said unto him, Verily I say unto thee, To day shalt thou be with me in paradise"(KJV, Lk 23:43). The answers as to actual knowing takes on many strange opinions and even for many a joyous celebration, which shivers the quiver to a shout. This is ever so evident when the saint knows that "Paradise," is synonymous with heaven being the house where God abode. There is the peculiarity with/within almost all religions as mortals attempt to explain this house as being an all encompassing heaven. Are we ever satisfied with an intangible?

The ethereal is always disconcerting. Deductively, if, the fly is above the knowledge of what we have obtained; then, the fly is as an effervesce of never existed. There are some in religion who goes as far as to giving God a planet. There is a possibility that God himself is the house: Is he the heaven? This may not be as preposterous as it may seem. The scriptures—Jesus says, "I am the door: by me if any man enter in, he shall be saved, and shall go in and out, and find pasture" (KJV, John 10:9). The best that can be said or stated is the fact this house is not like any house that we have visited at any point in our physicality. "In my father's house are many mansions, if it were not so, I would have told you" (KJV John 14:2). The transitions that allow the soul to rule—from God's love—do have many variations as God's mansions. Either way as to any, God's house—as to uncovering the essence of this home—is for the becoming acquainted with essence through its original self actualizations.

The pulsations are perforating on the inside help us to understand that our bodies too—**"here"**—are our houses. This is consequently realization nearing a full comprehension. Logical Deduction: If our body can be a house; then, God's body can also be a house.   On the other hand, God's house—in residency of spirit—is still beyond a complete understanding for the finite mind. Taking it from the word, God's "home or business" transcends. John on the isles of Patmos in an awe revelational moment referred to this of God this way:

The divine manifestations of the power of God! And from the throne proceeded Lightnings, thunderings, and voices. Seven lamps of fire were burning before the throne, which are the seven Spirits of God. Before the throne, there was a sea of glass, like crystal. And in the midst of the throne, and around the throne, were four living creatures full of eyes in front and in back (Revelation 4:5-6).

And of course in heaven, there was also the Devil. Jesus is the second part of the trinity—being this door spoke concerning the Devil losing his original position in this heavenly house of God said, "I beheld Satan as lightning fall from heaven" (KJV Luke 10:18). This house—this perfect house does not change—has plenty good room. Here is another thing one need to know about this house. This house has a presence that comes down from God, which receives all who would repent. The strongest proposition of all is that this is a heavenly devine propositions. Even, if Satan would repent, he too would be saved. As the master says, "As many as I love, I rebuke and chasten. Therefore be zealous and repent" (KJV, Rev 3:19). Repentance is the knock at the door, which allows an acquiescence into the house; where, all is welcome!

As we read, research, study, and stay with the general intent and in context of God's inner realm, Ezekiel has only begun to fear in the appreciation of being allowed to come here to God's house. It is useful to consider, however, the awesomeness of this place, this house, this house of God. With elevation of mind, reverence, trembling, and fear, we are—leap-frogged and carried with Ezekiel, as was Jacob—given a pictoria glimpse of and a Perspicacity view of this house as to spiritual import of Jacob as:

> Jacob awaked out of his sleep, and he said, Surely the LORD is in this place, and I knew it not. And he was afraid, and said, How dreadful is this place! This is none other but the house of God, and this is the gate of heaven (KJV Gen 28:16-17).

> "Again I say unto you, That if two of you shall agree on earth as touching any thing that they shall ask, it shall be done for them of my Father which is in heaven" (KJV, Mt. 18:19). Confirmation of two touching and agreeing confirms there is a house that is not made with hands awaits us at our time of transistion. As we move forward in this full import of the Ezekiel 47th chapter, with all that we have been through and with these pre-introductions, "the serving put on the dinner table" comes next. The next coming joy of eating the meat of the bone is when we begin to measure these waters, which ran out of God, from the "House of God." This house of God, let's just called it "heaven." For the present time, there are three house: Heaven for God, Earth for man, and Hell for the Devil[s] and all this was in the beginning. "In the beginning God created the Heaven and the earth (KJV Gen 1:1).

[w]aters issued out from under… & [t]he waters came down from under from… (KJV Ezekiel 47:1[l. 2-4]).

Water

"[W]aters issued out from under. . . & [t]he waters came down from under from. . . " (KJV Ezekiel 47:1, [l. 2-4]).

"But whosoever drinketh of the water that I shall give him shall never thirst; but the water that I shall give him shall be in him a well of water springing up into everlasting life" (KJV, Jn. 4:14). We have established that the relationship of water to the word of God is metaphorical [*a figure of speech*] in God's business of faith. The symbolism connotes strength and power. According to NOAA (n.d.), "The ocean covers 71 percent of the Earth's surface and contains 97 percent of the planet's water, yet more than 95 percent of the underwater world remains unexplored" (para. 1).[25] Just as everything, our bible suggests to us that water like all is of and from God. Biblically, John states he was given his sight in this regard: "And he shewed me a pure river of water of life, clear as crystal, proceeding out of the throne of God and of the Lamb" (KJV Rev 22:1).

Water is synonymous in the primary, and water is just water "wet and liquid" of the secondary. Whenever the word "water" is mentioned as to the primary, water refers to in most contexts the

---

[25] NOAA. "Oceans." NOAA: National Ocean and Atmospheric Administration. n. d. http://www.noaa.gov/ocean.html (accessed March 12, 2013).

contextual usage thereof as to and in a relationship with God the connective synonyms of (1) **The Lord**, (2) **The Word**, (3) **The Faith** (4) **The Spirit**, and (5) **The Life**. These waters are to be associated with the developing process and progress. In the forward movement of living, Ezekiel water in the correlation with humanity is biblically stated in scripture where, "Jesus answered and said unto her, If thou knewest the gift of God, and who it is that saith to thee, Give me to drink; thou wouldest have asked of him, and he would have given thee living water" (KJV,John 4:10). It is even now, which "the transmittable paradox of progress" water takes on the illogicality for the non-spiritual man and the illiberal lost. It is with the agreement that we start out accepting this water as the movement of God from the initial everything, even, beyond the all powerful now. It is in this agreement as this water commences to expand that Bible Study (2013) share with us Matthew Henry Commentary on Ezekiel the 47th chapter states:

> Most interpreters agree that these waters signify the gospel of Christ, which went forth from Jerusalem, and spread it into the countries about, and gifts and powers of the Holy Ghost which accompanied it, and by virtue of which it

spread far and produced strange and blessed effects (biblestudytools 2013).[26]

It is not by chance that "water" is a central argument that goes forth and further touching, even, our lives today. A chemical and biological importation to the primary shares with us the vivacity of "water" that comprises the majority of all life. While we're on the subject, let it be understood that we are 60% or more water at any given time. According to Przyborski & Wiscombe (2009), "The water, or hydrologic, cycle describes the pilgrimage of water as water molecules make their way from the Earth's surface to the atmosphere and back again, in some cases to below the surface" (para. 1).[27] In addition, it is common knowledge that 70% of the earth is water. Therefore, God use of water is clear. Water is the way to all that is of God and the workings of God. Understanding and knowing "water" is essential in the comprehension of "*The Paradox of* Evangelism's *Growth* " associated with our faith spill over as to so many types of religions is seeing and questioning the

[26] biblestudytools. "Matthew Henry Commentary on the Bible: Ezekiel 47." *Bible Study Tools*. 2013.
http://www.biblestudytools.com/commentaries/matthew-henry-complete/ezekiel/47.html (accessed February 17, 2013).

[27] Paul Przyborski & Warren Wiscombe. "A Multi-Phased Journey." *Nasa Earth Observatory*. 2009.
http://earthobservatory.nasa.gov/Features/Water/page2.php (accessed February 18, 2013).

what is "tares, and what is wheat" being the wrestle for humanity in these deep waters.

Water has flowed from the source for all to/ and within every religion inspite of man's rituals or sacred-cows—which does not exemption them from criticism—has us all *Wrestling In Deep Waters*. With infections, the paradox of growth proceed. Rituals are infections! Not willing to change in the appearance of new evidence of a non-truth associated with a thing is a disease relate to all reasoning. That which cannot be questioned or looked at objectively this too is a disease.

With Baptism and Purification, water delivers a blow to sacred-cows of do not touch, do not change, do not doubt, or do not attack. because the way we do a thing is how you get to heaven. Here is the paradox: Looking at the full gambit of each religious organization specifics, each for defining and separation reasons, looks nothing alike; yet, they all claim to be "right truth." That's a persistent "paradox," would you not say?

Some years ago, I visited a supposed Christian Church, and I was told by the pastor of this particular church these words: "If a man does not wash his feet of water when taking Lord's Supper, he will surely end up in Hell." Then, I asked, "What about the women?" I was told this: "Because of a woman's menstruation, they are already under the blood, and that blood cleanses them." Here looking at the water and being under water I better understand *Wrestling In Deep Waters.* The tares and wheat growing together create a great paradox. The absurdities that pervert God's word are pure nonesense. These absurities would be all laughable; except, there are misguided persons indoctrinated and dying without clue of what is right, living a lie of wrong.

God's water open our mind as to how water gives life and how water takes lives in the drowning similar association. It is fascinating how water is the driving force of all existence. In the careful study of scriptural information, God, in an instance of a spoken word, created everything from the beginning. And God said, Let there be light: and there was light"(KJV, Ge 1:3). This is literal in meaning as to everything, which encompasses all of the world's galaxies and all of God's Heavens. The Genesis account using a micro rendering to, no matter one's title, initially all comes from water. "And God. . . divided the waters which were under the firmament from the waters. . ."(KJV, Gen. 1:7).

It was not until the separations befell subtitles that we have our comprehensive understanding "to be" as physicals. "In the beginning God created the Heaven and earth. And, the earth was without form, and void and, darkness were upon the face of the deep. And the Spirit of God moved upon the face of the waters." (KJV Gen 1:1-2). According to Emoto (2001) in his book, *The Hidden Messages in Water* said, "If we attempt to think back before we became a human being, we would come to the conclusion that we existed as the water, we will get closer to finding the answer to the basic question what a human being is" (Prologue, p. xvii).[28]

The perplexity of water as to origination creates an overstatement; at the same time, this has created an understatement of the supposition. How can we see all with such limited present? As to all, we are left with only part-knowledge or part-comprehension on the first part without an invitation onto/ into as a transcendency? Even, Ezekiel in his transcending only saw what God wanted him to see. The much that he did see was a lot still not very much. The message is in the struggle of *Wrestling In Deep Waters*.

The old saying says, "Hindsight is 20/20;" but for Ezekiel, he saw in the foresight. This is still "in-part!" Scientists have shared with us, to the top of their ability life's derived theories. Still, there is countless the tons of water—as a cloud—floating above our heads as a daily reminder of the power of

---

[28] Emoto, Masaru. *The Hidden Messages in Water*. Edited by Beth Cardwell Hoyt. Translated by David A. Thayne. Hillboro, Oregon: Beyond Words Publishiing, 2004.

God. For sure and an assurance, the rain in nature's ways will unpack these clouds of the sky sending rain just to return again as water being the clouds. According to NOAA (n.d.) "One inch of rain over one square mile equals 17.4 million gallons of water weighing 143 million pounds (about 72,000 tons), or the weight of a train with 40 boxcars.[29] The scripture shares the introductory using Ezekiel and using us now: "Afterward he brought me again unto the door of the house; and, behold, waters. . ." (KJV Ezekiel 47:1, [l. 1-2]). Can it be stated beyond the stated as the clouds empty themselves as one does when going to the urinal—behold, water—behold, rain/water?

Whenever the waters break forth, life begins. The simplicity of the emitted is so overwhelming to, even, researchers will not endeavor to controvert. The contravention of water scientifically, and, otherwise, creates for all, as it did for Ezekiel, the assumption that water flows the more it grow in "The Evangelistic Growth's Paradox" of both "*Tares and Wheat.*" Water is not an assumption; it is a consumption. The production of such should never be an inconsistency. There is [at best] a viewable endurance; however, and without water, there could never have been no-consideration of the first

---

[29] NOAA. "Oceans." NOAA: National Ocean and Atmospheric Administration. n. d. http://www.noaa.gov/ocean.html (accessed March 12, 2013).

principle of life.   The inside, the outside, the around, and of everything that is living; there is water.

[w]aters issued out from under the threshold of the house eastward: for the forefront of the house stood toward the east, and... (KJV Ezekiel 47:1 [l. 2-3).

Threshold

"[W]aters issued out from under the threshold of the house eastward: for the forefront of the house stood toward the east, and..." (KJV Ezekiel 47:1 [l. 2-3).

To go throught "door" or come out of a "door," there has to be a "threshold" crossing. All other ways in and out is as a thief. Is this statement "threshold," in this 47th chapter of Ezekiel, of any significance? Well! Jesus said, " He that entereth not by the door into the sheepfold, but climbeth up some other way, the same is a thief and a robber" (KJV, Jn 10:1). In the structured idea of varying things, every word conveys a character of flavoring in the use associated with the substance.

It is the legality of the argument that we examine in varying degrees: just as a single word like the word "Threshold." Threshold is of importance in connection with God. The near full picture is always consistent with the scriptures. "Threshold is the sill of a door. This is a horizontal piece of wood or stone that forms the base of a doorway. The threshold offers the support to the passage throughway or doorway entrance to either entering or leaving a room or building; the space that a door can close" (Farlex 2013).[30] Therefore, in the 47th Chapter of Ezekiel, Ezekiel enters over "threshold" through the "door." The "water" is behind the "door." "God" holding the water. Then all of sudden "God" allows "water" to flow. This "water" flows first from around under the altar; then to "door," over the "threshold" and out the door. These are faith waters that start the happenings as a produced end product: a world and we that dwell herein.

The acquired importance of systematic separation of water in the leaving has to be the "from-where" We are at a point of being in the house, with God, before the altar, with an open door, and as water crosses the "threshold" thereof and therefrom. Once more, Matthew Henry commented on these threshold traveling waters and said, "The original of these waters was not aboveground, but they sprang up from under the threshold; for the fountain of a believer's life is a mystery."[31] In the calculated supplementary or

---

[30] Farlex. *Threshold: The Free Dictionary by Farlex.* 2013.
http://www.thefreedictionary.com/threshold (accessed February 22, 2013).

[31] biblestudytools. "Matthew Henry Commentary on the Bible: Ezekiel 47."
Bible Study Tools. 2013.
http://www.biblestudytools.com/commentaries/matthew-henry-complete/ezekiel/47.html (accessed February 22, 2013).

discriminant separability of the original state of the water (God's word) to the now Ezekiel shared experiences in the viewing of these waters (God's word) comes out as fire. Here, the water reaches the beginning journey, across the threshold out the door. Ezekiel, this 47th time is carried away for and observance where he saw the door opening. This door has a threshold attached to a forever house and is one in this instance with God as God forever issues forth these waters of faith.

God's constructed the threshold as he contructed "very" of all of his constructs. Your house has a threshold because God put a threshold in his house. Thresholds are either a beginning entrance or an ending exit. The weight of movement in the completed three-sixty begins and is of a place in God, which reaches a state of ending retreat back to a beginning. This beginning is the mouth of God—as if, it had never left God. This is how and why Ezekiel is here at this place as water begins to crossover the "Threshold."

"[T]he waters came down from under from the right side of the house, at the south side of the altar" (KJV Ezekiel 47:1)

Altar

"[T]he waters came down from under the right side of the house, at the south side of the altar"(KJV Ezekiel 47:1)

There is lot of meat on this old bone as a shock to a layman's comprehension in the places of God, with God, as God being God, and the "Alter." Ezekiel is here as God releases water from his altar. I thought this was strange until I went on to read scripture, which said, "He shall wash the inwards and the legs with water: and the priest shall bring it all, and burn it upon the altar: it is a burnt sacrifice, an offering made by fire, of a sweet savour unto the LORD" (KJV, Lev 1:13). Just another trancendency! Infinte v. Finite!

The altar of Ezekiel's text is God's Alter, which is above all the heavens; at the same time, God lives in a heaven that is his houses with the altar, the water, the worlds, and all the heavens. What a visual! This picture is God's magnificent picture, words are insufficient to illustrate or describe such to an understanding of clarity. This is just stabbing and jabbing at essence beyond all comprehension. Even, Holywood with every camera the world possesses could not come a close as to an exposure that would or could portray God magnificent as a glory of actuality. God alone is too much to encompass. Ask Moses and listen to what God told him concern his glory:

> Thou canst not see my face: for there shall no man see me, and live. And the LORD said, Behold, there is a place by me, and thou shalt stand upon a rock: And it shall come to pass, while my glory passeth by, that I will put thee in a clift of the rock, and will cover thee with my hand while I pass by: And I will take away mine hand, and thou shalt see my back parts: but my face shall not be seen (KJV, Ex 33:20-23).

To keep you turning the pages without screaming blaspheme, we are talking about multiple heavens, and heavens under water. Well! I did not say this; scripture says, "Praise him, ye heavens of heavens, and ye waters that [be] above the heavens"(KJV Psalms 148:4). This text's excerpted from the book of Ezekiel, as God shares with Ezekiel, is in no wise stating that Ezekiel ever saw the "glory of God" (God's all, God's everything, God's face). God does share with us the place where these "waters" are as beomg above the heavens. Logo rsuggests, if the water were above the heaven; then, the altar—God's Alter—is also above the water and the heavens because "the water came down from under the right side of the house at south side of the altar" (KJV Ezekiel 47:1). God in essence is indescribable other than to say, "GOD IS. . .."

However and simplistically, we are insufficient in our being to establish anything that God has done. The establishing of a layout—reading about the tares and the wheat—is the letting be and letting stand. The best that we can say in our "filling" is that God spiritual knowledge is our external pregnancy from the"altar" that flows into our wombs help us with our *Wrestling In Deep Waters*. *Wrestling In Deep Waters*, as this book is titled, is with us a "paradox" from the flow "that comes from the south side of the altar" (KJV Ezekiel 47:1) out from God's "door," over God's "threshold," and down to the "handlings of man" returns again to the glory of God.

God expands us as we go forth in the harvest from the "altar." "And before the throne [there was] a sea of glass like unto crystal: and in the midst of the throne, and round about the throne, [were] four beasts full of eyes before and behind"(KJV Rev. 4:6). According to Kandel (2003), which this author's concur: "All children love water; you too, I hope castles of clouds, invisible vapor, breaking water waves and spray, the calm of the ocean depths, peaceful lakes, rushing brooks, and the crystalline majesty of the glaciers. All is of water"

(p. xiii)!³²   These beautiful sweet waters get their beginning from God. The same is in us that produces life with us *Wrestling In Deep Waters*.

Just the mention of the word "altar" connotes and denotes the implied time without end of God as the "author and finisher of our faith" (KJV Heb 12:2). This is the symbolizing that "the word of God, shall stand for ever" (KJV Isa 40:8). The altar is the heart and soul of God's connectivity with his creatures. I specify creatures, rather than humans, because the word says, "The earth is the Lord's and fullness thereof" (KJV Psalms 24:1). It is at the altar that there was an authoring of water (word) from the south side in the Ezekiel commentary of his inclusion as we know that we are to rest in God and in his word.

While we are shouting, don't forget about the tares! The further "altering" with the building of man still gave and gives us the tares. To this God says, "They do always err in their heart; and they have not known my ways. So I swore in my wrath, They shall not enter into my rest" (KJV, Heb 3:10-11). The altar let the growth go forward starting with God just opening his mouth. Growth mixed the tares of man has given us this paradox, *Wrestling In Deep Waters*.

---

³² Kandel, R. S. (2003). Water From Heaven. Chichester, New York, U.S.A.: Columbia United Press.

The altar is the raised structure or place on which all sacrifices are offered to/for God. It is in this first state that God is that which comes forth as being that of him. This is the way man was made —"in God's image and after his likeness" (KJV Gen 1:26). The fact existence of the altar is as to the upholding maintenance from the image in the lifelong abiding that keeps us preaching the Gospel because the altar is alive. It is the eucharisticity where the altar is consecrated, which serves as the direct connection with God heart. God issued from himself—now comes the word as water—as water flowed along the south side of the altar. It is here where man receives, offers back, and up his liturgical expressions as praise to God in the form of a doxology.

As mystical as the all out of Ezekiel's experiences here in this 47th chapter, Ezekiel is beyond our literal as an experience. It has been suggested or advocated that this particular altar in this experience of Ezekiel (out of body experience) is God carrying Ezekiel again to a once in a lifetime contact with a living altar. The full proposal as it relates to everything that God creates has life forever in a connection with God. With the removal of God, the water would stops flowing. The rivers, lakes, and streams will dry up, and life would be no more— just a "Valley of Dry Bones." It is here, and then thereafter, comes the paradox from the growth that man over or under interprets the true intended of God.

From the altar, men build taking the flow of God's water and adapt it within their customs and fit the word to his own imagination and understanding.

This altar is where the water runs down from the south side across the threshold and out the door is an altar where God and God alone are permitted to vent here and where from. This altar is a place for offerings as God offers to us in the showing of Ezekiel his all. We are to offer back God our all. The word from the master himself proclaims and says, "[B]ehold, I come quickly; and my reward is with me, to give every man according as his work shall be. I am Alpha and Omega, the beginning and the end, the first and the last" (KJV, Rev. 22:12-13). God pours liberally out his water allows it to run along side of the altar "for" the feeding and the sustaining of us as we grow daily.

This is the view, which God shows Ezekiel, as the children of God complained, before the return to Jerusalem's altar. It's here for Ezekiel as to the gazing upon the altar. God delivers his message from the altar as a growing instrument. No human tongue can enumerate the favors that trace back to the telling God how he would have things to be. In captivity with burdens, the children of God turn and brought on themselves their circumstances, which caused God to carrying Ezekiel away and bring him back again to this altar.

WATERS GROWTH'S PARADOXICAL MEASUREMENTS

Water Away From the House

"To know" is the anticipation of the inclusion, the full segment of Ezekiel the 47th chapter that captures the growth of religion. These are the waters flowing away from the temple a thousand cubits. A thousand cubit is about a quarter of a mile. There is the defining of the man with the line in his hand, which should have come first as the "prelude" begins. In the abstract as a summary, it's just the mentioning of how these waters left the house and have grown looks at the paradoxes associated with these faiths' waters as metaphorical. It is the depth of these faiths' water that makes the magnitude as to our bonding connect the ancient, to the present, and to the future. It is with clarity that waters from around the altar of God have left these gates travelling, rising, and widening that soon to become a river. With meditation of the spirit, we are being entertained, as God's spiritual importation enriches our soul.

Ankle Deep Water; Ankle DeepReligion

And when the man that had the line in his hand went forth eastward, he measured a thousand cubits, and he brought me through the waters; the waters were to the ankles. (KJV, Ezekiel 47:3).

Linguistically, the rundown of the designated essence (water) intro of verse 3 is a count in spite of seemingly stated no count "the man. . ." refers to more than one in the counting, (Father, Son, & the Holy

Ghost as one in essence). *"And when the **man** that had the line in his hand went forth eastward..."* (KJV, Ezekiel 47:3). The same as to the prophets' notoriety of the past and the prophets of now. In the saying as to such, all prophets of God, in some respect or degree, gets an Ezekiel experience— of a sort—pertaining to and in their times regarding duties.

In the indirect, all acts or actions in the capacity of either, the triune of man (mind, body and soul) or the trinity of God (Father, Son, and Spirit), is the working of the three in agreement. John had a revelation, and he saw: "[A] new heaven and a new earth: for the first heaven and the first earth were passed away; and there was no more sea. And I John saw the holy city, new Jerusalem, coming down from God out of heaven, prepared as a bride adorned for her husband" (KJV, Rev. 21:1-2). This spiritual wrestling of John was in John as Ezekiel a growing as a mystery. The same with many other prophets and even the great prophet Paul was carried to a place while being in another place as a transcendence.

It is in Paul's second letter to the Corinthians that we see Paul experiencing prophetically the same as it was with Ezekiel as a commune with God. With much difficulty, it was impossible to let go; therefore, here Paul goes on and states:

And I knew such a man, (whether in the body, or out of the body, I cannot tell: God knoweth) How that he was caught up into paradise, and heard unspeakable words, which it is not lawful for a man to utter. Of such a one will I glory: yet of myself I will not glory, but in mine infirmities. For though I would desire to glory, I shall not be a fool; for I will say the truth: but now I forbear, lest any man should think of me above that which he seeth me to be, or that he heareth of me. And lest I should be exalted above measure through the abundance of the revelations, there was given to me a thorn in the flesh, the messenger of Satan to buffet me, lest I should be exalted above measure. For this thing, I be sought the Lord thrice that it might depart from me. And he said unto me, My grace is sufficient for thee: for my strength is made perfect in weakness. Most gladly, therefore, will I rather glory in my infirmities, that the power of Christ may rest upon me (KJV 2 Cor 12:3-9).

This is powerful stuff (God workings) and mind boggling, right? Would you believe it if I tell you that God is not through with nothing or nobody in these on-going flowings of waters? God is still working in the flow, in his own peculiar way, dealing with us— his peculiar people. God has always stretched forth his hand according to his own good pleasure. This may get another survey in this writing, at some point relating to importion; there is still much meat left on this old bone.

However, the reluctance to share is not that we do not know our place. *"Wrestling In Deep Waters* gives none an exemptions. The travel of these old faith waters are nowhere near exhausted, but in the movement of time these waters take us all to strange places, therefore, buckle up and fasten your seatbelt.

As to the arresting of our spirits, "the man with the line in hand" is not named in scripture, but who has the ability to clearly measured these faith's waters? Of course, we must accept this man as the son of God, in the spirit of God as one essence with the Father. The human embodiment of God for our understanding and comprehension is no new phenomena that us to pause in a head scratch. Ezekiel, as a catalyst in the spirit, shared with us from the times of old this now message. Faith-waters are only a metaphor for the growing word of mixed tares and wheat. To help us with our wrestle, God gave to us his only begotten Son, who essence qualifies him to measure these waters.

Humanity is only permitted to follow Jesus and the Holy Spirit, in the living. It is noteworthy to realize that God is handling Ezekiel as he is handling all of his creation. No one or anything is able to see the full glory of God and live. Ezekiel, like Mary Magdalene, and the other women who went to the tomb of Jesus were not specifically permitted to know who Jesus was, which seems to juxtapose the "the man with the line in hand." These all—and afterward—realized that this is the son of man [Jesus].

It is this "man with the line in his hand" taking and teaching Ezekiel and us in the experiential. Jesus did the same with Mary, so says the scripture, Mary thought Jesus to be the "gardener" (KJV John 20:13-14). Afterward, Jesus appeared to the brethren, but they did not recognize him at first, but later said, "Did not our heart burn within us, while he talked with us, by the way, and while he opened to us the scriptures" (KJV Luke 24:32)? The deep things of God are all within his word, and his word created everything with a constant searching; to the same, Jesus states, "I am he, which searcheth the reins and hearts, and I will give unto every one of you according to your works" (KJV Rev 2:23). Paul writes to the church at Corinth and says, "The Spirit searcheth all things, yea, and the deep things of God" (KJV 1 Corinthians. 2:10).

This fourth word "man" of the first line of the text Ezekiel 47:3 lives up in the metaphorical preamble to how "God dramatizes" his business. This is a drama praiseworthy that of an academy award. In the culminated, the pinnacle differentiates God [the soul of this reading] from the man needing this "man with the line in hand" standing between the gulf, *Wrestling In Deep Waters*. God puts understand in empty places. God explains, "For as the heavens are higher than the earth, so are my ways higher than your ways, and my thoughts than your thoughts" (KJV Isa 55:9). Is this "Enough said"?

God's ways are so high until he can come to one, and one will fall into unbelief as to what one's ears hear, and the mind will not know what the eyes have seen. Even here in the writing of this book, it is the things of the spirit as Paul says, "We speak not in the words which man's wisdom teacheth, but which the Holy Ghost teacheth; comparing spiritual things with spiritual" (KJV 1 Cor. 2:13). "[T]he man with the line in his hand" is incorporeal—and, yet, no ghost—measures the spiritual in the comparison of the spiritual and none spirital waters. This is the conclusion's application of excellence, which only God can apply without error. Only God can and has in the exercise thereof, "Declaring the end from the beginning, and from ancient times the things that are not yet done, saying, My counsel shall stand, and I will do all my pleasure" (KJV Isa 46:10). Koob 2010 says, "Bloom hypothesizes that "the pleasure we get from many things and activities is based in part on what we see as their essences."[33] Our pleasure to the seeing after, and God's pleasure to the seeing before.

In the finishing finale, let's say that the line, first of all, in the man's hand is not the finishing line. The man for Ezekiel's needs as a distinct character that he

---

[33] George F. Koob, Ph.D. *What Is Pleasure?* October 13, 2010. http://www.dana.org/news/cerebrum/detail.aspx?id=29196 (accessed August 7, 2013).

could identify with in his troubling thoughts: apples to apples and oranges to oranges. This is just the beginning of a journey; it's what the old folks use call "piece-way." When a visitor would come to say hello or spend a little time with one, at the end of the visitation, the old folks would say, "I will walk 'piece-ways' with you." They will sometime walk a quarter of a mile depending on how far away the person had come. This could be considered therapeutic. Walking is fantastic exercise. Walking and talking with another is comforting. "[T]he man with the line in his hand!" Walking and talking with the master is comforting!

"...[h]e measured a thousand cubits, and he brought me through the waters; the waters were to the ankles" (KJV, Ezekiel 47:3).

1st THOUSAND CUBITS

"He measured a thousand cubits, and he brought me through the waters; the waters were to the ankles" (KJV, Ezekiel 47: 3)

The captured commentary is no climax—"**a thousand cubits**." The captured commentary will use rhetorical succinctness—possibly, an impossibility. These waters are not so deep. This could be a hard blow for us, Ezekiel with his present ordeal, and the children of Israel, which is presently in captivity in a strange land. Much like the negro slavery of the old South. Not realizing it, this is still just *"Wrestling In Deep Waters."* This is not because of an imaginative stir with some elusive connection. This is because the power of God is the same with or without growth. Just, *Wresting In Deep Waters*!

On the part of man's growth, we must conclude that Ezekiel had accepted God because God only has the irrefutable answers to man's problems. The awesome import impact beginning point of the word is the water being metaphorical in this new comprehension. The forensics delve into the power of God from the altar before, during, and after the word leaves the house. The exploding out of the door over the threshold, now a stream, with water coming up to Ezekiel ankles—**A thousand cubits.** This thousand cubits is connected to our lives to the present day. A Thousand cubits is—for all understanding purposes— **"A QUARTER OF A MILE."** This is a seemingly short distance, but here— in this context of the text—canvases **"CENTURIES"** in the life living and altering of humanity. It is the internal reservoir of the soul that begs for understanding of these spiritually filling waters connected to the "quarter of a mile back to the door."

Let us not forget, this water is the word of God soon to be mixed with tares creating strange growth. This is not the quest of the text, but here is a pretext that appears to be edible and suitable for consumption before this man makes the first measurement. There was this young woman who decided to make for herself, "a dress." At the local fabric shop, she picks out her cloth; and, afterward, the seamstress makes her a dress. Further on down the stream of life, the seamstress measures again because things have changed from the first. The same seamstress, the same lady, but time in the progression thereof with this young woman had grown. Added pounds! Here, before "the thousand cubits, these waters" had not grown with but a little wrestling and no tares. This is God in our world before and prior to forming man from the dust of earth. Life skips over after a little intro to the next paragraph with Ezekiel and "the man with line in his hand" where these waters are up Ezekiel's ankles.

What is most important about the before denotation relative to Ezekiel is the wording of the scripture, which rightly do not include Ezekiel, "*And when the man that had the line in his hand went forth eastward...*" Ez 47:3; however, Ezekiel is accompanying the man "*brought me through the waters; the waters were to the ankles*" (KJV, Ezekiel 47:3). This is where the beginning experience of this present world's man gets his beginning. However, before the "these waters were to the ankles" (Ez.43:3) and before there were "Adam and Eve." There were other God's creatures. To this God asked, "Where were you when I laid the foundations of the earth. . . ? Who laid its cornerstone, when the morning stars sang together, and all the sons of God shouted with joy?" (KJV Job 38:4, 6-7). There were the "Morning Stars" and the "Sons of God"(angels) who saw the creation of our worlds and galaxies. It is here the water—before Ezekiel and "the man with line in his hand"—was the word that God used in his directing and communication with his other creatures and worlds, and therefrom made them.

It is without argumentation that there are other worlds—other than our. If any wish to deny such: you have a hole in your head. It is only the sickos that see the world as 4,000 yrs. The earth is billions of years old and there other celestial bodies older than the earth. It is the proposition of other worlds and worldly activities in other galaxies that embrace the waters of Ezekiel text before the thousand cubits (a quarter of a mile) from the house. There is the scientific evidence that meteorites have fallen to the earth that are 4 billion years older than the earth.[34] Are we alone? This is a matter of conjecture. The scripture says, "Hath in these last days spoken unto us by his Son, whom he

---

[34] Stardate. "Meteorites." *StarDate*. n.d. http://stardate.org/astro-guide/ssguide/meteorites (accessed March 2, 2013).

hath appointed heir of all things, by whom also he made the **worlds**" (KJV Heb 1:2). And, it is here the word "worlds" is plural. You say we believe our bible, what say we as to this?

The water has run out from under the door. The house is no longer flooded. Ezekiel and "the man with the line his hand" are a thousand cubits (a quarter of a mile) down river. You do know about "down river?" You know, contrary to Jack and Jill going up hill for water that water runs down stream, right? The word is never in vain because God's spoken word always accomplishes the intended. Here is some good food for thought: Peter says, "Beloved, be not ignorant of this one thing, that one day is with the Lord as a thousand years, and a thousand years as one day"(KJV 2 Peter 3:8).

The difficulty for most of us is in the fact that we attempt to juxtapose (put side by side) too much in an association to what God would do in a given particular. You know, we like to put God's mind right next to our mind with our "big" thoughts (LOL). Remember God said this to the prophets, "For as the heavens are higher than the earth, so are my ways higher than your ways, and my thoughts than your thoughts" (KJV, Isa 55:9).

Daily as learning being, God reveal more and more of himself unto us. This is our duty learning;

however, there is nothing for God to learn: "knowing the end from the beginning." God has always known what he knows, and he knows everything, even, before it happens. Furthermore, it does not happen unless he allows it to happen. "[M]y ways [are] higher than your ways, and my thoughts than your thoughts" (Isa. 55:9).

It is of a struggle grabbing hold of something; and, suddenly, you want to let go of that thing and you can't. This is what *Wrestling In Deep Waters* is all about. When Jacob got a hold to this something he said, "I am not going to let go, until [God], you bless me." (KJV, Gen 32:26). Oh! What a wrestle—doing the something and the something is doing us: in and out as we keep hold on waiting the blessing.

This is the way it is with this "A" portion of our text, which captures the mind's eye of thought as one grapples with the lesser particle out of God's mind of omniscience. For identification and analogy, this lesser is less than the "gnat" to God, but enough to create a world. This is the same as time itself, which is just a tiny particle hued out of eternity for man's convenience, which just so happens to be nothing to God. But, and, whenever time becomes full, God always trouble these old faith waters. God's word gave us his spirit. "But when the fulness of the time was come, God sent forth his Son, made of a woman, made under the law; To redeem them that were under the law, that we might receive the adoption of sons" (KJV, Gal 4:4-5).

The water from the beginning to this thousand cubits of Ezekiel experience is far reaching beyond any human finite comprehension. However, one can look at particles of time in the water. God's man, Ezekiel, shared an overview. Let's see this water as word in the struggle as purposed. The learning and training in the word of God create God's emissaries, God's representatives, God's envoys, God's ambassadors, God's messengers, God's agents, and God's angels to help man while he *Wrestling in Deep Waters.* Water in the first thousand cubits is antiquity's past. It is here in the before, which precludedthe creation of the earth finds God through his word was busy.

It seems that God was molding and shaping man in him. Yet, at the same time, in this intervening space of eternal time, God had the man and the woman in a non revealed state. This world was not yet created, but God knew exactly what all will be and what all will do. "According as he hath chosen us in him before the foundation of the world, that we should be holy and without blame before him in love" (KJV Eph 1:4). Here the word had already worked out everything before the "when or the where." This is why God had said, "Before I formed thee in the belly I knew thee; and before thou camest

forth out of the womb I sanctified thee, and I ordained thee a prophet unto the nations" (KJV, Jer 1:5).

This thousand cubits beginning is also of a
thousand cubits that is up to the ankle of
Ezekiel. It is here in the beginning that God said
to Himself, His Son, and His Spirit, "Let there be!"
and "Let Us!" From the "Let Us" scripture says,
"God created man in his own image, in the image
of God created he him; male and female created
he them" (KJV Gen 1:27). This is the beginning
of thousand cubits away from the house. There is a
message here: One should rule one house well; One
should make one house the house of prayer; but,
great works most often take place away from the
house from down off the mountaintop in the
valley. In the valley, life is produced. If, there is
"no valley love; no fruit for the offering, these waters
are just dirty." These old waters are plenty dirty.
This is why there is this continued "*Wrestling In Deep
Dirty Waters.*" It is a hard and lonely bed with no
fruit. Here, these waters are getting ready to grow.
As God begins to speak, life gets a base and is set in
motion to produce more life.

Here is another take on this word of God that
can help us with our ministry as we swim up stream in
these old muddy waters. God's word submitted to us
and another is also time sensitive. This is to say
that God alone is the only with the day, the hour, and

the year of the word's solidification. Peter helps us with understand when he says, "Be not ignorant of this one thing, that one day is with the Lord as a thousand years, and a thousand years as one day" (KJV2 Peter 3:8). It is "the-as-to" that will always be of a supposition relative to an undefinable specific time. However, skipping forward, the inclusions can be established as to the creativity within frames. As a result, this allows us an introspection starting with the "thousand cubits." It is this examination, which will allow some details of the mental involvement between God and his creation. This particular is to the "tares and wheat." This word of God mixed man's word is evangelistic and grows various paradoxes; therefore, "Hear instruction and be wise, and do not disdain it" (NKJV, Pr 8:33). "And God blessed them, saying, Be fruitful, and multiply, and fill the waters in the seas, and let fowl multiply in the earth" (KJV, Gen. 1:22).

As we get older in the growing, things do not get easier of itself, neither better. Children and grandchildren seem to create a deeper growing sets of circumstances. These keeps up holding on and depending on God as we wrestle in these waters. In the initial from the beginning it was all so simple— then and there. Ezekiel is now, and, here with God, "the man with the line in his hand" measuring these waters. God created us after his likeness and in his image receives and is added to the word. The word, the water, of a thousand cubits coming only up to the ankle of Ezekiel is, easier, discerned as unadulterated being as what God intended for man. This time frame is still of antiquity and beyond archeological find; whereas, an inclusion traps the Garden of Eden to the end of the flood and Norah. This is as to religion— "ankle deep water and religion." Let us not forget that only God can measure his word, and only God can separate the "*tares*" from the "*wheat*." The scriptures say, "Let both grow together until the harvest: and at the time of harvest I will say to the reapers, Gather ye together first the tares, and bind them in bundles to burn them: but gather the wheat into my barn" (KJV Matt 13:30). Tares cannot plant themselves; there has to be a sower.   Daily, humanity is bombarded with misinformation disguised as the truth. Evil knows no rest, and evil loves sowing bad seed—"tares." If it were not for the tares planted by the evilness of man, we would have smooth sailing. We would not be *Wrestling In Deep Waters* of any kind. This sower of tares gets a start from a connecting to the nature of Satan—the Devil himself. "*Tares*" are synonymous with lies. God says this concerning the Devil, "When he speaketh a lie, he speaketh of his own: for he is a liar, and the father of it" (KJV, John 8:44). Now, whose your "daddy?" LOL!!! As a consequence, the first "Tares" sown "were" the lies whispered in

Eve ears. God told Adam and Eve that they could eat of every tree in the garden, except, the tree in the midst of Garden. At the point of eating thereof, they would surely die, but "[t]he serpent [Satan] said unto the woman, Ye shall not surely die"(KJV, Gen 3:4). Eve was beguiled; Eve did eat of sin's fruit down in the "middle" of the garden among he the other "tree parts of the garden."

Eve was shame begins the blame game. Shame has a way of not wanting to be alone. I know you know what I am talking about, and you too have been there once or twice. "Shame" will become clever in the convincing another to do the same to cover shame by shaming. We are bed fellows now; if laughter, we are not laughing at one another.

Eve convinced Adam to eat, and Adam did eat, and humanity has gone the way of the grave ever since. These waters were still, but, up to the ankle. The "Tares," of this first quarter of a mile [the thousand cubits], had not mightly infectioned the bloodline of humanity. As we know, life is in the blood, right? From the time of Eve and Adam's sin, tblood became tainted and unclean. The word says, "For I will cleanse their blood that I have not cleansed..."(KJV Joel 3:21). This little infection still allowed man to live up to the ripe old age of 900 years. The shame, without the further incoming sin of man, has these waters only up to Ezekiel ankles. This is the first thousand cubits downstream.

Ezekiel has been taught much by God and is seeing much in the water. Ezekiel and the children are still in captivity. Ezekiel was a captive and a prophet during the seventy-year period of the Babylonian Captivity, all because of sins. However, it is here that Ezekiel is walking with "the man with the line in his hand" to measure these first thousand cubits where water is up to his ankle. Ezekiel was only thirty years of age (30) when he started his prophetic commission. This was the same age of Jesus when he began is ministry. Ezekiel learned and was taught by God according to forty-six text of God involvement with his people—in the cleansing aspects of their lives. At this point, the 47th chapter of Ezekiel is the after of information connected with the prior knowledge given to Ezekiel by God. Least we forget, information directly from God is "Good News;" even—and when, we do not like the consequences or the message. "The sower may mistake and sow his peas crookedly: the peas make no mistake, but come up and show his line." - Ralph Waldo Emerson[35]

In the midst of the thousand cubits, the sower of the tares has corrupted the seed. It is here for Ezekiel understanding, as a prophet, to first be introduced to the historicity of humanity's falling.

---

[35] Stephanie Sarkis, Ph.D. "50 Quotes on Consequences." Psychology Today. April 22, 2012. ww.psychologytoday.com/blog/here-there-and-everywhere/201204/50-quotes-consequences (accessed March 16, 2013).

This is no fluke or flop! We can stop the press and state for a front page headline: "Humanity Has Fallen!" Grave as all of this might be, from this point forward, God's heart will continue to ache grievingly to regret that he ever made man and allowed there to be a humanity. It could be here, the place, where "the man with line in hand" and Ezekiel in the measuring of these waters, which comes, only, as high as the ankles. It is here we read the sciputre, which says, "And it repented the LORD that he had made man on the earth, and it grieved him at his heart" (KJV Genesis 6:6).

Conceptualizing the far distance, the quarter of a mile from the beginning of God's word had very little pollution. These waters do continue to travel, grow, and deepens. Here and wherein, we come to the realization that there are two sides to God. The God of Love and the God of Wrath. This is what keeps Ezekiel humble and we the same. God allows us to go only so far; and, then, God has to exercise his prerogative, getting our attention, helps us understand that we are not all of that.

Looking at this "man with the line in his hand" and Ezekiel, these waters only came up to the ankle. Ankle Deep Religion! Ankle Growth Tares. Ankle Growth of Wheat. Ankle Deep Waters. It is here the text of Ezekiel is metaphoric as to the symbolic usage of water as an emblem in this motif flow of God's word. **Pin the following, if you will, and we will get back to**

this later: "Many have drown in ankle deep water." Here with the initial tares of ankle deep water flooded Adam and Eve from the "Garden of Eden!" The "Wheat" in these ankle deep waters gave birth to the boys Able and Cain. These same waters, which measured up to the ankle also gave "Tares," which cause Cain to kill Able, ushered in murder.

History's antiquity of the first thousand cubits had to amaze Ezekiel in such an unfathomable way in this first hand visualization of God's glorious works. If there were a way for one to transpose self, the awe of Ezekiel would be our awe in this very instance. What grasp us most in the interposition of Ezekiel experience, *Wrestling In Deep Waters?* Or, would the amazement overshadow the elucidation? Or, would the revelation overwhelm to confusion? These questions raised are of much spiritual piercing natures. The involved of these cubits in Ezekiel depictions—and the measured water cubits to follow —are of such paramount inclusion as an in part, but, yield to us no satisfactory absolute of itself.

This places us at the point terminable with the first bad seed, which pictured humanity as to the almost status, in our minds, as being gods. Giants walked the land of the fallen angels taking to themselves humanity's nature and sperm-ed evil unbearable, even, beyond the tolerance of God. In this modern era, "in the Philippines, a giant human skeleton was found measuring 17 feet long."[36] "The sons of God [Fallen angels] saw the daughters of men that they were fair; and they took them wives of all which they chose" (KJV, Genesis 6:2).

The *Tares and Wheat,* in the measuring of these waters, which only comes up to the ankles, is breathtaking to say the least. *"Tares and Wheat"* is the drama made for television. Ezekiel gets the supported role as God plays himself as the "All" in an actual portrayal of "God's Real-Time" as God stretches forth his hand flooding the earth.

It is here in this real-time that we here reach back grabbing the previously stated: [*Of the pinned as promised:* "**Many have drown in ankle deep water.**"]. As to the pinned, God drowned virtually all of humanity except for Noah and the inhabitants of the Ark. These waters were only a thousand cubits from the gate of God's house which only came up to the ankles. Ankle deep water flooded an entire planet called earth. "[T]he man with the line of his hand" measured a thousand cubits and the water came up only to the ankle. Imagine what a river of water released by God would do. This would be for real *Wrestling In Deep Waters.*

[36] 6000year.org. "Giants." 6000years.org: Amazing Bible Discoveries. n.d. http://www.6000years.org/frame.php?page=giants (accessed March 17, 2013).

The majority of us would like our children, grandchildren, and offsprings to be as close as possible to the word of God as a life's alignment while *Wrestling In Deep Waters*. This being so, we can point and say, "That's my boy or that's my girl!" God wants to view humanity as not struggling with their *Wrestling In Deep Waters*. It is here and now that God is carrying us in these deep waters.

Clearly, humanity has disappointed God in this first thousand cubits as these waters were only ankle-deep. Down through the many years beginning with the Beguiling of Eve, evil has been sowing tares among the wheat. "The field is the world; the good seed are the children of the kingdom; but the tares are the children of the wicked one; The enemy that sowed them is the devil; the harvest is the end of the world; and the reapers are the angels" (KJV Matt 13:38-39). It is quite understandable—since "evil" is in competition with "good;" consequently, more the "good" so will be more the "evil." In other words, the more planted wheat; the more planted tares. It is to be understood that evil is always present, ask Paul:

> For I know that in me (that is, in my flesh,) dwelleth no good thing: for to will is present with me; but how to perform that which is good I find not. For the good that I would I do not: but the

evil which I would not, that I do. Now if I do that I would not, it is no more I that do it, but sin that dwelleth in me. I find then a law, that, when I would do good, evil is present with me (KJV, Rom. 7:18-21).

With easy understanding, God was then, God is now, and God will forever be God. Satan, the devil, and the fallen Angels are of the created that came afterward as a caught-up wanting to be God. God was the first evangelist with a correct word that spoke into existence life. Satan knows the word of God, and Satan has many evangelists today that have taken over many pulpits and polluting God's word and way. Demons take God's word and perverted the word for selfish gain sowing tares among the wheat. "But when the blade [wheat] was sprung up, and brought forth fruit, then appeared the tares also"(KJV Matt 13:26).

There is no need for an all out debate as to anyone really knowing specifics about anything that God only knows relating to the knowing of time. In the text, "*The man that had the line in his hand went forth eastward, he measured a thousand cubits, and he brought me through the waters; the waters were to the ankles*" (KJV, Ezekiel 47:3), we must not forget that time is relative to God. This is clear from reading of the scriptures; whereas, scripture encourages us, "To be not ignorant of this one thing, that one day is with the Lord as a thousand years, and a thousand years as one day"(KJV2 Peter 3: 8) as a repeated in the reminding.

The confusion is everywhere and Christians are allowing the demon possessed evangelists to persuade them that the field of science is wrong and evil to make themselves some shining figure. It works this way: when you don't know you don't others to know because of your insecurity and inferiority. This is where, even, a christian should not be afraid of science. It is of a truth and fact that just this planet is billions of years old. Now back to the time issue of no debate, according to Simmons (2009), "A marked bone which was probably used as a record of months and lunar phases and which was from approximately 9000 to 8001 BC or as late as 6500 BC was found in Ishango, which is now Zaire" (para 2).[37] It is here in the "Tares and Wheat"—Biblically or Scientifically—we are talking about years beyond the billion, which include Eve and the flood. We can point back with documentation to Eve, but there is further pointing and Ezekiel has a mighty standing in the midst of the waters that only comes up to his ankles.

---

[37] Simmons, Lorna. "Ancient Time Keepers." University Lowbrow Astronomers. June 2009.
http://www.umich.edu/~lowbrows/reflections/1999/lsimmons.2.html (accessed March 17, 2013).

The Devil showed himself to Eve, and Eve saw for the first time the perception of vanity. Eve took and put the vanity that she saw, in her mouth, in the dark of night. Once in the mouth of Eve, she continued to eat. This forbidden fruit, which sprang up from earth's nature, fertilized the emotional nature of Eve to sin's lay [pathos won—inserting the emotional ecstasy of sin, which Eve did take in]. As, if Eve had not done enough on her own accord, she bent the wrist of Adam persuading him to eat and enjoy the fruit that the Devil gave her in the darkness of night. Finally, it is here—and, now with boldness—they both did eat in the garden and in the sight of all God's creatures, "shame seized the unseen." And Adam said to God, "I heard thy voice in the garden, and I was afraid, because I was naked; and I hid myself" (KJV Ge 3:10).

Here, this chapter closes with another dispensation beginning to become filled with the tares (pervert words and half truths) of the "you shall not die" lie. Just as the activism of the handsome and beautiful of this present day. Is there or is there not "Aids?" The night is still filled with darkness! Turning the page, there will be more! This is about as real as it gets; babes beware! The waters are going to become a little deeper, but it is still the same old *"Wrestling In Deep Waters."*

Adventuring into the exploration of the dispensations associated with these old faith waters, our travelling from God's internals to his externals tied eternity will be our focus; as, we continue *Wrestling In Deep Waters.*

1st THOUSAND CUBITS

Man's Innocent

Let's just think: can we give man any credit for anything other than the wrong he has commited? The answer will come later. First, on our own, let's enjoy these various scripture in text and context: Gen. 1:26; Gen. 2:16,17; Gen. 3:6; Gen. 3:22-24. However, if you want to just keep reading and come back later, this too will finds us wading in these waters that come up to our ankles. Ezekiel's vision of these waters coming up to the ankles is with "the man with the line in his hand" measuring these faith's waters. Naïveness is the life's blindness of the perfect man—the man of innocence.

It is here that man was made both male and female, and there was not a schism in the body. "So God created man in his own image, in the image of God created he him; male and female created he them" (KJV Ge 1:27). Man was made to sleep, and God extracted the female from the one body and made two similar-dissimilar bodies. I am under the opinion if you are one of the readers of this book; you are of age possessing the intellect's comprehension of "similar-dissimilar bodies." Therefore, there is no need to keep beating that old, dead horse to death.

For now, this is the entertaining, and the intellectual will come later for the inspection. The pedagogic importation is the nerdy filtered of the last part minuscule boredom, which we are not about. God excites and is exciting. Even here in the dispensation of "Man's Innocent," there is an excitement. I know some of us do not appreciate innocence and believe such is a waste. The only reason that we think that way is because we ourselves cannot go back to the days of "then or when." You know—If I "coulda," " woulda," " shoulda." Allow me with the little youth that still left in me to say this to you, "That's just a "bucket of water" under the bridge!" It is here, as we progress, we are headed for the river where there will be lot's of —"*Wrestling In Deep Waters.*"

I am still transitioning as I "*Wrestling In Deep Waters*" with an attempt to enter the traveling around of "Man's Innocent." Beforehand, I submit to us that God knew the next. This is why God said, in his word, immediately after creating man, "Be fruitful and multiply" (KJV Ge 1:28). I say, "Even, as to the parleying between Satan and Eve, there was for a moment— innocence. Nevertheless, Eve in her continued parleying with the snake—the night creeper, the tempter, and the devil—who is always up to no good— in innocence received a compromise.

Without getting ahead of ourselves—"Lost Innocence will come in the next unit"—the "Innocent of Man" was so pronounced and domineering until even "Lamb and Lion" was at peace with God's authority. Once more there will come a time that all will respect God's authority to the point of: "The wolf also shall dwell with the lamb, and the leopard shall lie down with the kid; and the calf and the young lion and the fatling together; and a little child shall lead them" (KJV, Isa 11:6).

However, in the beginning, God's word that has travelled these one thousand cubits is God will. It was for us that God in his will of the flowing word said:

Let us make man in our image, after our likeness: and let them have dominion over the fish of the sea, and over the fowl of the air, and over the cattle, and over all the earth, and over every creeping thing that creepeth upon the earth (KJV Ge 1:26).

As a sidebar, we will get back to those days of innocence where according to scripture says, "And the cow and the bear shall feed; their young ones shall lie down together: and the lion shall eat straw like the ox" (KJV Isa 11:7). It is with God's word we journey on to the next with the realization that as long as there is the darkness of night, the garden will have a night creeper sowing bad seeds to be reaped by the unsuspecting.

"Again he measured a thousand, and brought me through the waters; the waters were to the knees. Again he measured a thousand, and brought me through; the waters were to the loins" (KJV, Ezekiel 47:4).

2st THOUSAND CUBITS

"Again he measured a thousand, and brought me through the waters; the waters were to the knees" (KJV, Ezekiel 47:4)

Looking at the picture below, these waters here seem to be waters that is purified as they appear to be crystal clear. These waters look so serene and beautiful! This is the profundity of God's word in true faith. God's word is of crystal clarity, cleanness, and

clearness. This is a biblical narrative sparkling unambiguously with freshness. However, this painting of God to the understanding with Ezekiel is clear, and it is sharp. These faith waters are spiritually deep by themselves but become physical deepened with the inclusion of man's word. The mind's image from scripture relating to the picture makes the outdoors person want to get to these waters for a bit of camping and fishing. This is Beautiful; isn't it? This picture of these almost flawless and picture perfect waters is God's way of showing his grace and his perfection. There is no need for another insertion from us. We only need to share in loving with one another as we *"Wrestling In Deep Water,"* letting go and letting God's love flow on the inside growing us for better days to come.

Here, *"Again he measured a thousand, and brought me through the waters; the waters were to the knees.* (KJV, Ezekiel 47:4). These waters have deepened; they have grown, which will be as to measuring an anomaly within the faith: God's "wheat"and more of sinful "tares!" Tares and wheat are the subjects from the time of departure of these waters from the alter that pit God against the Devil; whereas, Jesus said, "I beheld Satan as lightning fall from heaven" (KJV Luke 10:18).

And yet, very shortly after his creation, for some profoundly unknown reason, there arose within him [Satan] the first sin, a sin that brought about his personal fall from his endowed position and a sin that was destined to blight the new creation and bring depravity to the race. So speedily it happened (Embrace The Truth n. d.).[38]

These waters—now measures much deeper! The adage of another thousand cubits carried Ezekiel another quarter of a mile downstream. Adding the first to the second, the picture painted sees "the man with the line and in his hand" and Ezekiel a half a mile out, from the gates in these faith's waters. This is only an assumption question [not meant to be an absolute or dogma as to a point]. I know we should never look back. However, I think it would be logical that we offer these waters more than just for a once-over. Having said that, presenting a presumption doubt or question. Here now is the question: Is it a possibility that the between of God's house and the gates —this was Satan residency as the closest to God at the time? Satan was beyond all, except the excellence of God. Satan original position was one of leading exaltation. Satan was kicked out of God's Heaven, and his own station of aboard. Mockingly, the seeing of this happened, the scripture also asked a most piercing question: "How art thou fallen from heaven, O Lucifer, son of

---

[38] Embrace The Truth. "Theology > Sin > Reality of Satan > Fall from Heaven." Embraced by Truth...Reflections on Theology and Life. n. d. http://www.embracedbytruth.com/Sin/Reality%20of%20Satan/Fall%20from%20Heaven.htm (accessed March 18, 2013).

the morning! How art thou, cut down to the ground, which didst weaken the nations" (KJV Isa. 14:12)? This had to make a data imprint in human's existence. This is where the tares became tangled with the wheat. The Devil has never had any power or authority; other than, power someone gives him. There would be "more power in the life of the saved with "Less" tares; if, the save would not give up their power to the Devil.

These teaching waters two thousand cubits from the gate. This is the quarter-mile added to the first— "the man with the line in his hand" with water up to Ezekiel knees. We only surmise to "this man with the line in a hand," is, O. K.? I say this because honestly we are not told his name. However, the question and to us is this: who is it that is qualified to measure these faiths within us? Just asking! Further, just trying to simplify as an opening of the second dispensation; these measured waters are up to the knees.

Wrestling In Deep Waters" can be enjoyable, as well as, inspirational for spirit filled soldier of God. Only in the,"Keep it simple, stupid. Just mumbling to me, O. K.!'"

2st THOUSAND CUBITS

Man of Conscience

Gen. 3:7, 22; Gen. 6:5, 11-12; Gen. 7:11-12, 23.

This is the a complex opening of the second dispensation; the measuring of these waters up the knees as we grasp the humility of Ezekiel's thoughts. This creates a place pointed! Much of the old is also the new, "Good and Evil!" Life of the old was not so recorded and intellectually defined as to the new with now our speed of communications. The drives of the tribe as to demographic philosophies are those of the Conservatives, Moderateness, and Liberalism! They were as are! They were just not penned. However, all have always been present. All these were of antiquity, which now juxtaposes modern times claiming humility.

It can be said that these beliefs are acting from a clean, clear, and moral conscious. But, Really? Friedrich Nietzsche stated: "communal solidarity is annihilated by the highest and strongest drives that, when they break out passionately, whip the individual

far past the average low level of the 'herd-conscience.[39]
Not trying to demonstrate any kind of advantage
"intellectually, the lesson is a little shared "Ethos"
beneficially supported by its points. This is normally
true when the individual is a distinguished scholar.
Suddenly there is this shift. Bear in mind, we
are talking about faith and not some out space alien
falling to the earth surviving. We are talking
about the word of God; and, we are talking
about a progress to all because of the word coming
down. Of course, each of these measurements is
the measurements of dispensations. "Water up
to the ankles and now waters up to the knees!" The
second in the line of the dispensations—the beginning
"Conscience of man."

Further along downstream in the river's
flow, these ripples in the waters will become
much more excited. That's kind of preachy; isn't it?
<u>Ripples in the water!</u> It was eating in the night,
beginning with the wrong food, created the first
ripple. Eve and Adam could have eaten any and
everything in the garden except that forbidden fruit
of the middle nature that rose them to conscience.
Now ashamed, they hid and dressed their nakedness.
Scripture looks God-ward and states, "Neither is
there any creature that is not manifest in his sight:
<u>but all things are naked</u> and opened unto the eyes of

[39] Friedrich Nietzsche "The Origins of Herd Morality" in P Singer (ed). *Ethics.*
Oxford University Press. NY 1994

with whom we have to do" (KJV Heb 4:13). Conscience says, "We all have sinned. . . ." Those of no conscience is never wrong to themselves. This is why one can shoot another and later rejoice. They only look upon the power of their depravity juxtaposed to nothing else; therefore, they are always right in their own mind with their own opinions. So and now, there is a ripple in the water. This ripple is associated with "the conscience of man," [this second status of man's allotment, dispensationally] is what caused these waters of faith to rise to "the knees."

The metaphorical measuring of these waters in this text of Ezekiel (lest we forget) is growth's paradox relating to the conscience of man—as the man being used by Satan—plants tares among the wheat. Conscience at this point is the beginning as an issue for the downfall of man. These waters are not so calm at this point. However, Matthew Henry says, "Before the sea was and when there were no depths in which the waters were gathered together, no fountains from which those waters might arise, none of that deep on which the Spirit of God moved for the production of the visible creation".[40] Progress is good; nevertheless,

_____

[40] (from Matthew Henry's Commentary on the Whole Bible: New Modern Edition, Electronic Database. Copyright (c) 1991 by Hendrickson Publishers, Inc.)

there is this planting of tares in the night by the enemy, which disrupts the flow of serenity.

Do we not know that sin can cause disruptions? With the planted tares in the lives of Adam and Eve (first conscious beginning), Adam and Eve were kicked out of their home (the Garden of Eden) with their first state privileges repossessed (disruption). We do know that sin as tares can cause you to lose everything in a twinkling of an eye? God in our—lives just as it was in the lives of Adam and Eve—will act in accordance with our status. So says the scripture, "God drove out the man; and he placed at the east of the garden of Eden Cherubim's, and a flaming sword which turned every way, to keep the way of the tree of life" (KJV Ge 3:24).

In the state of man's conscience, humanity begins to reproduce. The darkness is seemingly filled with no longer a shame, which inserts a continuing series of discipline for the female [birth's pain] and for the man [tilling the ground for survival]. After all of this, there came death.

> And Adam lived a hundred and thirty years, and begat a son in his own likeness, after his image; and called his name Seth: And the days of Adam after he had begotten Seth was eight hundred years: and he begat sons and daughters: And all the days that Adam lived were nine hundred and thirty years: and he died (KJV Ge 5:3-5).

After procreation and the institution of death, it is humanity in this conscious state that muddied these trusted waters that Ezekiel sees that comes up to the knees. This made God sad that he ever made man. The scripture says:

> And it repented the LORD that he had made man on the earth, and it grieved him at his heart. And the LORD said, I will destroy man whom I have created from the face of the earth; both man, and beast, and the creeping thing, and the fowls of the air; for it repented me that I have made them (KJV, Ge 6:6-7).

The dispensation of the following power ushered in a kind of "affluenza" that caused one brother to take the life of another, and today the killings continue looming in the dark craves of time. The jealousy over the gift of another is a counterfeit seed sown. Tares among Wheat! Death is usually the result. Cain Killed Able! The "affluenza" of trying to keep up with what the Joneses have, from the death of Able, continues to affect God's creation. The wishing for more money coveting the possession of others. The dispensation of the first power ushered in a kind of "affluenza" that caused one brother to shed the blood of the other, and today the killings continue to appear within the sinister gaps of evil men's occasions.

It is the repeated measuring these waters a second time "another thousand cubits" has much water under the bridge. These waters are up to the knees. Image that you can drown in ankle deep water, what you say about "water up to our knees." This is what knee deep waters produces: "And now art thou cursed from the earth, which hath opened her mouth to receive thy brother's blood from thy hand" (KJV Ge 4:11). The purity of the instruction given is mixed with a deadly blood. It is understandable why the scripture says, "And it repented the LORD that he had made man on the earth, and it grieved him at his heart" (KJV Gen. 6:6). The "Conscience of Man" climaxes in the first state of a new beginning. The Devil and the Sons of God (fallen angels) took unto them wives of men allowed wickedness of every kind upon the face of the earth. And, the scripture says:

> That the sons of God saw the daughters of men that they were fair; and they took them wives of all which they chose. And the LORD said, My spirit shall not always strive with man, for that he also is flesh: yet his days shall be a hundred and twenty years. There were giants in the earth in those days; and also after that, when the sons of God came in unto the daughters of men, and they bare children to them, the same became mighty men which were of old, men of renown.

And GOD saw that the wickedness of man was great in the earth, and that every imagination of the thoughts of his heart was only evil continually. And it repented the LORD that he had made man on the earth, and it grieved him at his heart. And the LORD said, I will destroy man whom I have created from the face of the earth; both man, and beast, and the creeping thing, and the fowls of the air; for it repenteth me that I have made them. But Noah found grace in the eyes of the LORD (KJV Ge 6:2-8).

There is no conclusion other than what the preacher says, "Fear God, and keep his commandments: for this is the whole duty of man" (KJV, Ecc 12:13).

3rd THOUSAND CUBITS

"Again he measured a thousand and brought me through; the waters were to the loins" (KJV, Ezekiel 47:4)

These waters have gotten a little rougher, and these waters are up to the loins. Navigation can be a little more difficult because these waters have gotten much deeper. Here, this *Wrestling In Deep Waters* is one of not allowing the current from every wind of doctrine sweep us off our feet. "Again he measured a thousand, and brought me through; the waters were to the loins" (KJV, Ezekiel 47:4). These are grown folk waters! It is down the stream, with

Paul, we understand the rise of these old waters. Always bear in mind, where there is plenty water, these waters will be turbulent, and don't forget the wind. Satan is "prince of the power of the air" (KJV, Eph. 2:2). And Paul said to us, "[H]enceforth be no more children, tossed to and fro, and carried about with every wind of doctrine, by the sleight of men, and cunning craftiness, whereby they lie in wait to deceive; but speaking the truth in love, may grow up into him in all things, which is the head, even Christ" (KJV, Eph 4:14-15). This is very important; since, we as Christians are in the business of rescuing and bringing others to God. WRT (2013) says, "After learning techniques for swimming, wading, throwing ropes and rescuing people in relatively easy rapids, you will refine and gain expertise with these skills in a variety of bigger rapids and more complex situations."[41]

Time in God's dispensation is of many years progressed into and with humanities' quests. With understanding and reasoning, we are fully aware there have been many "Tares" sown among the "Wheat." Mama says, "It is hard for me to know when you are telling me the truth." Mama went on to say, "Since

---

[41] Boreal River. "WHITEWATER RESCUE TECHNICIAN (WRT) – 4 DAYS." *Boreal River*. 2013. http://borealriver.com/boreal-river-rescue-whitewater-swiftwater-training/technician-wrt-4days/ (accessed May 29, 2013).

the Bible said, 'Withhold, not correction from the child: for if thou beatest him with the rod, he shall not die. Thou shalt beat him with the rod and shalt deliver his soul from hell' (KJV Prov. 23:13-14); I am going to whip your behind just in case.'" Mama did not play, and, neither does God!

"[T]he man with line in his hand" has measured another thousand cubits, three quarters of a mile. God is talking to Ezekiel in his mind. It is the many things that are beyond Ezekiel—and, even I—that all can never be all written in a book as a literal word. It is the following along in the comprehending just as it was when God moved when: "Darkness was upon the face of the deep. And the Spirit of God moved upon the face of the waters" (KJV, Gen. 1:2). And Jesus went to say as to this position of what deliverance says, "For it is not ye that speak, but the Spirit of your Father, which speaketh in you" (KJV, Mt 10:20). So now, where are we? We are in the third dispensation where "man has authority over the earth:" See Gen. 9: 1, 2; Gen. 11: 1- 4; Gen. 11:5-8. And, we add, this is "**man under promise**" to "the-mix" in this same chapter. This is the fourth dispensation of patriarchal times, which also includes "**man under promise:**" See Gen. 12:1-3; Gen. 13:14-17; Gen. 15:5; Gen. 26:3; Gen. 28:12-13; Exod. 1: 13-14. These waters are up to the "Lions." Having said that, it is utterly impossible to cover everything as to these two dispensations. Suffice it that we get a sweeping overview to know that God is in these deep waters with us as we continue *"Wrestling In Deep Waters."*

All of us have read or heard about the flood that consumed the earth; however these dispensations come after the recovery as a new beginning; whereas, scriptures says, "And God blessed Noah and his sons, and said unto them, Be fruitful, and multiply, and replenish the earth" (KJV, Ge 9:1). As with all new beginning, we start out with the right motives as to everything. We are going to walk up right. We are not going to lie. We are going to give God all the glory. Not too long after this new beginning—where water seems to settle—snakes begin to crawl and show their heads in these old muddy waters. We wrestle on!

This is essential to bear in mind, God told Noah to get two of every creature upon on earth to carry in the boat. We know that Satan is a "snake." I will submit to us that one of the snakes that went to the Ark was the devil. Recall the story of the "frozen snake:" There was a man walking along the way, headed home. A voice out of nowhere said, "Mister, Mister save me." The man being startled looked here and there, saw no one stated, "Who is it?" The snake down in the ice on the ground near frozen to death replied, "Down here Mister!" The man snapped and said, "Oh, you snake!" The snake said, "Yes, me! Will you help me?" The man said, "How can I help you?"

The snake said, "Pick me up and put me in your upper-body and take me home with you to keep me from freezing to death." The man said, "But, you are a snake, and you will bite me." The snake cunning as he has always, said tenderly to the man, "No, Mister, I will never bite you." As the story goes and continues, the man took the snake home in his upper-body and placed the snake by his warm fire. The snake throbbed out. Immediately, the snake bit the man. The man said, to the snake, "I thought that you said that would not bite me." The snake said, "I did; but, remember, I am a snake."

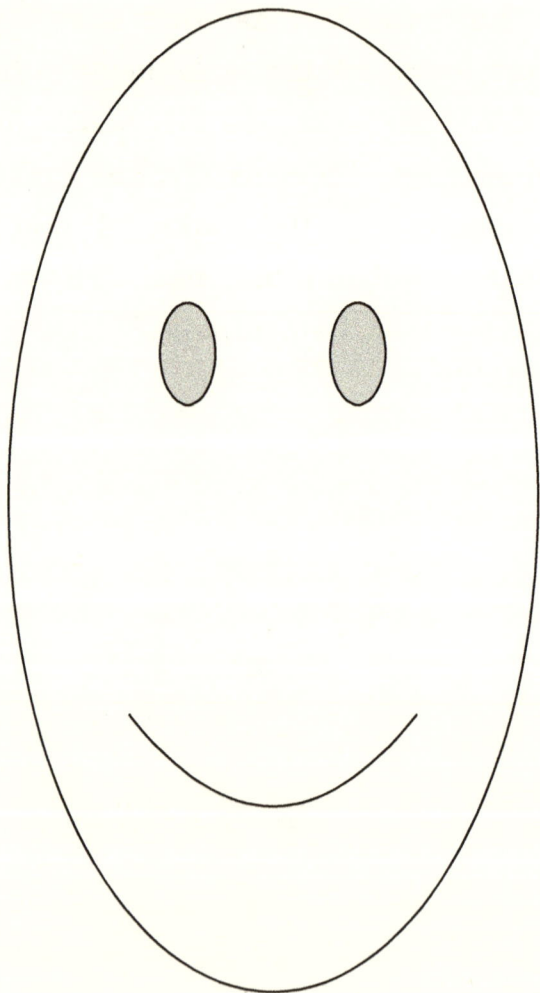

3rd THOUSAND CUBITS

Man's Authority Over the Earth

Gen. 9: 1, 2; Gen. 11: 1-4; Gen. 11:5-8

Oh, what a terrific job we have done these many years [facetiously speaking] having authority over the earth. We can consider ourselves "the world greatest takers." This is where folly begins, "taking," as to what is power and might. Coupled with writing, I love to read, especially, philosophy and the Bible! Throughout much of "Man Authority Over the Earth," man has concentrated on warfare as a means to dominate, usurping authority. Herder (1800) in his writings, *Outlines of a Philosophy of the History of Man,* concerning man's plight in his authoritative capacity asked, "Why was it denied thee, thou great, thou matchless, Hannibal, to prevent the country's ruin, and march directly to the wolf's den of the hereditary foe, immediately after the battle Cannae?"[42] As an

---

[42] Herder, Johann Gottfried. *Outlines of a Philosophy of the History of Man.* New York: Bergman Publishers, 1800.

employee, man—as an authoritarian over the earth—
has majored in the folly of sin and has minored in the
goodness of God. Dispensations or no dispensations,
the evidences spread themselves from Cain to Iraq
onto every hilltop, in every valley saturated with
everything associated with death and destruction.

These waters are little deeper, now; they reach
up to the lions. Many years ago Jimmy Cliff had a
song that stated, "I can see clearly now that the rain is
gone" because even with all of the rain these waters
only comes up to the lions. This is three fourth of a
mile from the beginning. There are measurings and
there are "Measurements" just as there is the
day, and there are the "Days!" The scripture
says, "But, beloved, be not ignorant of this one
thing, that one day is with the Lord as a thousand
years, and a thousand years as one day" (KJV 2 Peter
3:8). In this dispensation, "Man's Authority Over
the Earth" is in these waters, which only come up
to the waist (lions). Depending on the current swift
transition, these were sweeping struggles, "*Wrestling
In Deep Waters.*" It is here that man once more
exceeds his authority and to such:

> The LORD came down to see the city and the
> tower, which the children of men builded. And
> the LORD said, Behold, the people is one, and
> they have all one language; and this they begin
> to do: and now nothing will be restrained from

them, which they have imagined doing. Go to, let us go down, and there confound their language that they may not understand one another's speech. So the LORD scattered them abroad from thence upon the face of all the earth: and they left off to build the city. Therefore is the name of it called Babel; because the LORD did there confound the language of all the earth: and from thence did the LORD scatter them abroad upon the face of all the earth (KJV Ge 11:5-9).

The evidence was/is certainly clear as to the much planted "tares" among the "wheat" by the devil and man in his beginning authority over the earth. It has always been of human's pride and arrogance with giving man authority over anything. For the Christian, *"Wrestling In Deep Waters"* is a righteous fight against the vile. This is where half truths attempt a dictate and begin warring in our members against truth. Hammer (1945) stated:

> Truth comes from the Deity and is dispersed through myriads of intelligences, gradually reaching men distorted and dimmed. The Source is pure, but flows through imperfect and polluted channels, as the Fountain of truth has many tributaries. Then too, the human mind is so constituted that it can perceive only a fragment

of truth at a time, and that fragment faintly. Just as the naked eye cannot gaze directly at the dazzling sun, so the mind of man cannot behold truth without being veiled (p. 45).[43]

It is here the waters of life are troubled and are mixed with turbulence, which keeps humanity, *"Wrestling In Deep Waters."* Now that, the language of man is confused; this means that problems solved, right? Wrong, Wrong— Wrong! For a period of time, relating to every transition, there can be a comfort zone shielded by the intended. This is the waters with a soothing sound as it runs over the rocks before a troubling wave. These are they that disrupt the comfort of sleep. This too may be a good thing because "[a] little sleep, a little slumber, and a little folding of the hands to sleep— So shall your poverty come on you like a prowler" (NKJV Pr 6:10-11). Once these faith waters get their depths, the "grove's cuts" are forever, which await only a filling. Over time—believe you me, the precipitation of life's waters will provide this filling. There are many pollutants in the air; it is the precipitation that brings those these pollutants in the "grove's cuts," fills the cracks. Therefore, and for now, these waters are no longer so clean despite the depth.

---

[43] Hammer, Frank L. *Life and Its Mysteries*. Forgotten Books, 1945.

3rd THOUSAND CUBITS

Man Under Promise

Gen. 12:1-3; Gen. 13:14-17; Gen. 15:5; Gen. 26:3; Gen. 28:12-13; Exod. 1: 13-14.

In the midst of these waters, we are no different than those struggling men (renown or not) of antiquity; as to when they first excerpt their authority over the earth, they too had a trying time *"Wrestling In Deep Waters."* Now these waters are the same, let just see how long it took for man—in his confused language state— to get back to the previous state of disobedience. Looking onto the next page of life, *Wrestling In Deep Waters* moves us into a fourth dispensation. It is here—these waters are still up to the waist (lions). As we know, from time to time, when it rains, it seems as if the rain is "pouring down." It is here, at and in these times, that the waters of faith are but up to the waist. Here in the constancy of eternity, this rise is in turbulent times above the waist to only settling back to the waist. This is the height of one's struggle *Wrestling in Deep Waters* as to a suddenness. This suddennes might be: an unexpected death of a love one, some sickness, or some other catastrophe that is unrelentingly. These waters pulsate as a rise above their normal level, excitedly, and then drops suddenly to an original state of "waist deep waters."

Man under promise was from Babel to the Sinai; the man had a duty to believe God as his promise. The scripture goes on to say, "Blessed be the LORD that hath given rest unto his people Israel, according to all that he promised: there hath not failed one word of all his good promise, which he promised by the hand of Moses his servant" (KJV, 1Ki 8:56). However, Israel like many of us today rejected God's grace and, conceitedly, took upon themselves the weight of the law. It is where a yoke got placed about the neck of the Israelites which neither their fathers nor succeeding humanity were unable to bear. This went further as "Israel pursued the law claiming righteousness. However through the law—Israel, like others, was not able to remain righteousness. Why? "Because they did not seek it by faith— but as it were, by the works of the law. For they stumbled at that stumbling stone" (KJV Rom. 9:31-33).

It is here in the heavy walk of the word that we continue with Ezekiel in the measuring of these waters mixed with tares and wheat, *"Wrestling In Deep Waters."* The knowledge is heavy that caused a violation chronological structure with the above inclusion of a "piece-bit" of the fifth dispensation, which is to come. Yet, and, however, we are here continuing to look into and address many centuries of many years of rising waters. These waters are up to the waist now. Ezekiel is looking with us with the help of God, in our "third heaven's capture." Accepting this *"Wrestling Deep Waters"* narrative, unequivocally Ezekiel was in or out of the body. Stated again, God has the power to do whatever he pleases.

For entertainment and preadventure, since we have already included a chronological violation according to the dispensations of life, let's skip to several views of "third heaven experiences." These experiences should serve as the backdrop for Ezekiel is going through of our text. These "third heaven experiences" is the understand of the preachers of now when they do not understand themselves. These "third heaven experiences" of biblical scriptures are of the power and prerogative of God as to his previlege in the "omni" of his essence. It is here to the said that God "Having made known unto us the mystery of his will, according to his good pleasure which he hath purposed in himself: That in the dispensation of the fulness of times he might gather together in one all things in Christ, both which are in heaven, and which are on earth. . ." (KJV, Eph 1:9-10).

Third Heaven Experiences

How do we explain these "third heaven experiences"? Has God taken you in some exordinary experienced way out yourself into another understanding that you cannot explain? It was stated by one sometime ago and they said, "This happens more than you would imagine, but when it does happen the one it happens too he/she keeps usually one's mouth close not to want to seem like a lunatic." Image the following as to this being you:

I. "And Jacob called the name of the place Peniel: for I have seen God face to face, and my life is preserved" (KJV, Ge 32:30).

II. "Then Nebuchadnezzar the king was astonished, and rose up in haste, and spake, and said unto his counselors, Did not we cast three men bound into the midst of the fire? They answered and said unto the king, True, O king. He answered and said, Lo, I see four men loose, walking in the midst of the fire, and they have no hurt; and the form of the fourth is like the Son of God" (KJV, Dan. 3:24-25)

III. "In the year that king Uzziah died I saw also the Lord sitting upon a throne, high and lifted up, and his train filled the temple"(KJV Isa 6:1)

IV. "I knew a man in Christ above fourteen years ago, (whether in the body, I cannot tell; or whether out of the body, I cannot tell: God knoweth;) such a one caught up to the third heaven" (KJV2 Co 12:2).

4th THOUSAND CUBITS

"Afterward he measured a thousand; and it was a river that I could not pass over: for the waters had risen, waters to swim in, a river that could not be passed over" (KJV, Ezekiel 47:5)

The River

This fourth thousand cubits away from the beginning is now one mile. These waters got started a long time ago. These waters were before the making of man and will forever flow. After the flood, Noah left the ark. It is here at the receding of the flood waters we have now this river that is a mile away from the start of these waters. However, it is now in the marathon running we have come a full mile. The scripture looks at these waters, and the lives of the human family and said, "Wherefore, seeing we also are compassed about with so great a cloud of witnesses, let us lay aside every weight, and the sin which doth so easily beset us, and let us run with patience the race that is set before us" (KJV, Heb 12:1).

It is—under the dispensation of the law, leaving the Sinai—we have birth of Christ who obeyed God and keep his commandments. We all know the story. Israel again and again dumps God in the going after many other dumb idol gods. Israel was the prodigal son—just as the children of so many of us today— living and eating in "hog-pens." This is an extraordinarily deep, wide river. As the old song goes, "Still waters run deep." However, these waters that we are wrestling in/with are anything but "still." These waters at the measurement of "one mile" from the start is a deep river. This river is too deep to stand up in, and it is too wide for the average swimmer to swim from one side to the other without some type of assistance. "God is our refuge and strength, a very present help in trouble" (KJV , Ps 46:1).

As to our life's present state, this river, these mixed waters, is the gulf between God and us because of the implantation of the tares among the wheat. This gulf is older than the forty-two (42) generation that is between the old testament and the new testament where God refused to have direct talks with man. However, the man still had his law. The scripture looked at this absent period of God and said, "But before faith came, we were kept under the law, shut up unto the faith which should afterwards be revealed. Therefore, the law was our schoolmaster to bring us unto Christ that we might be justified by faith" (KJV, Gal 3:23-24).

This river is polluted to nearing the core of disruption with these mixtures of "tares and wheat." Growth of these waters as to being a river is one of life's greatest paradox. Evangelically, the prophets received their messages directly from God. It is here and therein that these messengers of God—prophets and priests with the written law —were some of the most leading evil doers under the law. "But they cried out, away with him, away with him, crucify him. Pilate saith unto them, shall I crucify your King? The chief priest answered, we have no king but Caesar" (KJV, Jn 19:15). There have been given to us many pictures and symbolisms relating to these waters of life leading us to the river. If you like, you can call this river, Jordan! As a side bar for stability absent of illusion and delusion, verse 9 of this 47th chapter of Ezekiel gives us clarity:

And it shall come to pass that everything that liveth, which moveth, whithersoever the rivers shall come, shall live: and there shall be a very great multitude of fish because these waters shall come thither: for they shall be healed, and everything shall live whither the river cometh (KJV Eze 47:9).

Listen, at the river there is nothing to be afraid of because God has the last say as to everything, even, onto the crossing over. The crossover is another chapter as to the going into another book to be published. Whenever, "God troubles waters" there is usually a breakthrough and a crossing over. This is the transition when God take our hand with us walking with him on these old dirty waters. Shout!

What God showed to Ezekiel and shows us is that getting to the river is not that difficult because we all get there, even though, there are "tares among wheat" in the continued growing. The evangelistic growth's paradox of this all is the have to allow both "tares and wheat" to grow together. These two, "tares and wheat," are the swelling of the river with disturbing currents that flow during harvest time. As stated, getting to the river is not difficult, but, the navigation of the river in our life, one must trust God.

This river (the Jordon) is symbolic of the waters of our faith's trial and tribulation as we continue in the favor of God receiving eternal life.

"*Wrestling In Deep Waters*" is all about—"tares and wheat, trials, and tribulations with in the middle of river. The "tares mixed with wheat has caused us suffering with trials and tribulations in a river that has peaked and is a serious obstacle in the life of the living. The tangible metaphors association with and as to these troubling waters give us additionally the metaphor, Jordon, as point of crossover. At the time of harvest, the Jordan swelled to an impassable width of over one mile, which is fifty time wider than its norm (for Jordan overflowing all banks all the time at the time of harvest). See Joshua 3:1-6; 14-17.

It is here after we have jumped the clock relating to chronological order that we are about to return to the point of dispensation's synchronization. Look at this this way, remember the movie, "Fallen" starring Denzel Washington where the "Devil" escaped death by leap-frogging from the body of "Denzel" to the body of a "pussycat" meandered of to enter another victim. This scene was the beginning of the movie, which was the last of the movie. In a flickering flash, the movie, "Fallen" retro-ed to the start with a two-hour movie to this same point of the "Devil" entering the cat. This is the same as to the coming of the dispensation, "Man under the Law." Wrestling In Deep Waters, has given us a end-view of things to come as we now dwelve in man's depravity under the law.

4th THOUSAND CUBITS

Man Under the Law

Exod. 19:1-8; 2 Kings 17:1-18; 2 Kings 25: 1 -11; Acts 2:22-23; Acts 7:5152; Rom. 3:19-20; Rom. 10:5; Gal. 3: 10.)

Before the law, during the period of the law, and after the law, the infinite (God) created man with the power of his word. However, God goes silent for 400 years between the Old Testament and the New Testament. Man loses his powers in the disconnect. God refused to speak to the man. However, as to the time before the establishment of the "Thou Shall Not [s]," God spoke to the children of Israel from the clouds. Being under the influenced understanding, the benefits were—as to living life— for the children of Israel was an up vector. The clouds are up; heaven is up; the Lord sits ["up"]; Jesus is up sits on the right side of power making intercession for us 24/7; and, hell is below. The downs of life are of/from the rigidity of a law, which left "man under the law" not many alternative.

As a practical matter, the ending is a slidetoward the dawn. This time called the process of circumvention. Before walking heavily into this "law business of the Israelites," let me share with you an excerpt that I feel is compelling. Smith (2011) says, "There are thirty-three (33) ways God speaks to man" (para. 1). Smith goes on to share with us those ways, which are as follows:

> 1. Verbal Communication - an internal, inaudible message through a word or words spoken through the still, small voice of God, or perhaps, on occasion, the <u>audible</u> voice of God. This communication could be a specific Scripture, a statement, a question, a command. The "still small voice" in 1 Kings 19:12 can also be translated "the sound of gentle stillness" or "a gentle whisper; " the Hebrew is literally "a voice, a small whisper."
>
> 2. Mental Pictures - inner picture-images or symbols, or messages as parables; a picture flashed across the inner screen of our mind.
>
> 3. Encounter - a phenomenal experience with God without words, but leaving an overwhelming message or strong impression.
>
> 4. Vision - a series of pictorial messages or visual images, literal or symbolic, while awake. These may require some additional reflective and prayerful interpretation.
>
> 5. Dream - a series of pictorial messages or visual images, literal or symbolic, while asleep. There

are two formats of dreams — these dreams arising from the subconscious mind that God uses to convey a message and dreams that are directly heaven-sent from God. Dreams may require some additional reflective and prayerful interpretation.

6. Intellectual Reasoning- cognitive, mental processing and evaluating of data leading to clear conclusions like connecting pieces of a puzzle.

7. Imagination - inner images or concepts creatively conceived or formed through guided imagery.

8. Intuitively or intuition - knowing the right thing to do or say is about the spontaneous

9. Conscience - knowing the right from wrong. See Romans 2:15; 9:1.

10. Thoughts - ideas or principles, words or pictures that grow with increasing awareness, clarity, unfolding, intensity, conviction, or volume in the mind.

11. Emotions - a gut-level feeling, desire, impulse, impression, arresting concern, or insistent nudge.

12. Memory - the remembrance of an event, thought, or Scripture previously learned. See John 2:22; 14:26.

13. Common Sense - the ordinary use of rational, good judgment through experience and logical thinking.

14. Observation - a quickening of insight when observing or reflecting on people, art or

inanimate objects. For Scriptural examples of listening to God by observing inanimate objects, see Jeremiah and the potter's wheel in Jeremiah 18:1-10, Amos and the plumb line in Amos 7:7-8, Saul and Samuel's torn cloak in 1 Samuel 15:27-28.

15. Liturgy - a ritual ceremony or observance that emphasizes or drives home a certain reality or truth.

16. Nature - the silent shouting of God's creation, or inner messages that occur through ordinary created objects such as a flower or a tree. See Psalm 19:1-4.

17. Circumstances - confirming situations and events that all seem to point in the same direction often combined with a profound sense of inner peace. See Colossians 3:15.

18. Signs and Wonders - external, more dramatic, supernatural and visible demonstrations of God's love and power to help, heal, care or deliver.

19. Pain - physical suffering serving as God's megaphone to gain our attention or teach some lesson.

20. Angels - messengers from God.

21. Theophany - a visible manifestation of God bringing a message. See Exodus 3:1-6.

22. Tongues and Interpretation - a spontaneous message from God in an unlearned language with interpretation in order to speak incisively to a situation, or bring immediate and profound comfort and peace to a person in distress.

23. Word of Wisdom - an appropriate, instantaneous insight for a particular occasion, to make a right decision, to discern good from evil, or to resolve, help or heal a particular situation or need.

24. Word of Knowledge - a fragment of knowledge or disclosure of truth implanted by God — not learned through the mind — about a particular person or situation for a specific purpose.

25. Prophecy - a timely message or utterance through an individual from God to strengthen, encourage or comfort that person or that group of people at that particular time. See 1 Corinthians 14:3.

26. Music - meditative or worshipful music that brings stillness, a sense of God's presence, or a spirit of praise.

27. Bible - the holy, super-slow, spiritual reading and application of the Scriptures, and can include using the five senses of sight, hearing, smell, taste, and touch. This is sometimes described as "reading with the mind in the heart." The written revelation of God's Word is combined with the way the Holy Spirit quickens particular portions as a direct word in a present circumstance.

28. Meditation - memorization, repetition and prayerful rumination of Scripture texts.

29. Devotional Classics - a holy, super-slow reading of spiritual writings.

30. Journaling - writing down times of communion or conversations with God.

31. Soul Friends - spiritual guides, godly friends or spouses who provide spiritual direction and counsel.

32. Collective Voice - the united voice and decision made by a group of believers.

33. Preaching and Teaching - public presentation of the Word of God and applied by the Holy Spirit to the individual.[44]

Therefore, the initialization of law had God voice directing Israel in their daily affairs.

The is noteworthy—as an understanding, understanding the law—in the chieftain referring to that part of the law, as of/coming from God; we refer to these as the "Thou Shall Not [s]. . . ." We all know that the Old Testament has hundreds of laws and ritual; whereas, the "Thou Shall Not [s]. . ." are only ten (10). Lest we forget, this book is about *Wrestling In Deep Waters*; and, these waters are faith's waters; and, these waters have become a river. It is how, under the law, these faith's waters became a river that is significant.

The man under the law—or just a man—has had a hard time submitting to God and his authority without wanting to help God out. The man in the trying to help God out has sown many "tares" of the

[44] Smith, David John. "How Does God Speak to Us? 33 Ways from Faith That Takes." *shelboese.org*. 2011. http://shelboese.org/how-does-god-speak-to-us-33-ways/ (accessed June 3, 2013).

enemy (Satan). You have heard it said many times, "I know what I should be doing, but you don't know what I am going through." The aforesaid statement is the same as to what the children of Israel did and were saying. They knew what was right, but—and, because of unbalance in their lives they did according to their natural natures, and their interactions agreed with their fleshly other. Paul said it best:

> For I know that in me (that is, in my flesh,) dwelleth no good thing: for to0 will is pres-ent with me; but how to perform that which is good I find not. For the good that I would I do not: but the evil which I would not—that I do. Now if I do that I would not, it is no more I that do it, but sin that dwelleth in me. I find then a law, that, when I would do good, evil is present with me. For I delight in the law of God after the inward man. But —I see another law in my members, warring against the law of my mind, and bringing me into captivity to the law of sin, which is in my members. O wretched man that I am! Who shall deliver me from the body of this death (KJV, Rom 7:18-24)?

It is here with the little that Paul says is the total functioning of sin, which cause the law to be such a burden and was never a "means to an end." This idiom "means to an end" point to the insufficiency of the law. The instrumentality of the law that was given to Israel numerous prophets received the unadulterated word from God to assist Israel with the law, but with no lasting reward. The word, the wheat, these waters are over the head of Ezekiel.

These waters are mixed tares and wheat as the paradox of evangelism's growth presist back as a command under the law to the river as a stated:

> Now go, write it before them in a table, and note it in a book, that it may be for the time to come for ever and ever: That this is a rebellious people, lying children, children that will not hear the law of the LORD: Which say to the seers, See not; and to the prophets, Prophesy not unto us right things, speak unto us smooth things, prophesy deceits: Get you out of the way, turn aside out of the path, cause the Holy One of Israel to cease from before us. Wherefore thus saith the Holy One of Israel, Because ye despise this word, and trust in oppression and perverseness, and stay thereon: Therefore this iniquity shall be to you as a breach ready to fall, swelling out in a high wall, whose breaking cometh suddenly at an instant (KJV Isa 30:8-13).

The Israelites were given much insight to what law should be; but as to violations, "Man Under the Law" was divorced from God. This insight —for the most part—was Israel's misfortunes. Scripture says, " But they did not obey nor incline their ear, but made their neck stiff, that they might not hear nor receive instruction" (KJV Jer 17:23). This was the continued wrestling that Israel was having as they tried to carry the burden of the law around their necks. The more they tried to serve law the more flesh got in the way. The convenience of near self rule it was the existence of the flesh in Israel's behavior that gave God's children their great *Wrestling In Deep Waters*. Even now, God wants Israel saved from the shame of the fact that He had divorce them for their unfaithfulness. Will you accept, even in our live and in our times, divorce is because unfaithfulness relating to something: un-Godliness, money, fame, or shame.

Treading these treacherous waters with "Man Under the Law's" dispensation—it is here the more we realize that the law was a burden. The burden of the law is fact that it caused Israel to fall into a state of unfaithfulness with having no true recourse for repentance. These waters have risen high, and the law is too difficult for God's children. Someone said the other day that "laws are made by man to be changed by man." Let us bear in mind this famous quote of old honest abe:

Let me not be understood as saying that there are no bad laws, nor that grievances may not arise for the redress of which no legal provisions have been made. I mean to say no such thing. But I do mean to say that although bad laws, if they exist, should be repealed as soon as possible, still, while they continue in force, for the sake of example they should be religiously observed.

Abraham Lincoln (1809 - 1865)

Israel were a stiff-necked people and did not like change; therefore, every ritual and law became religious observance. There were the Sabbaths—Deut 5:15, the New Moons—Num 10:10; Lev 23:24-25; 1 Sam 20:5-6, 29; 2 Kings 4:23, and many types of Sacrifices. These, themselves, were the burdens of the so called law of Israel.

4th THOUSAND CUBITS

Four Hundred Years of Silence

God is consistent as to the similitude of man, in the sense, God forgives and forget, but God also grieves. "And it repented the LORD that he had made man on the earth, and it grieved him at his heart" (KJV, Gen. 6:6). Finally, and here now, God is so disappointed with man until he has quit talking to the prophets. However, God had set the stage for culminating activities to take place doing these 400 years of silence. This period is the leading up period as to we having a savior. These years are the years in Ezekiel experience of a water measured to deep to stand up in and too wide to cross.

Ezekiel as a prophet of God receives an encompassed look at this Jorden; as well as, many other prophets in the climaxing work of God, especially, during this 400 years of seemingly silence. It is, according to Kirkpatrick (n. d.), we are presenting the prophets' look associated with this 400 year period stated:

Daniel completed his interpretation of Nebuchadnezzar's dream with the following prophecy: "Thou sawest till that a stone was cut out without hands, which smote the image upon his feet that were of iron and clay, and brake them in pieces" (KJV Daniel 2:34). The stone cut out without hands is Christ Jesus. Then Daniel continues: "Then was the iron, the clay, the brass, the silver, and the gold, broken to pieces together, and became like the chaff of the summer threshing floor; and the wind carried them away, that no place was found for them: and the stone that smote the image became a great mountain, and filled the whole earth" (KJV Daniel 2:35).

Thus, the kingdoms represented in Nebuchadnezzar's dream come to their end, and Jesus Christ, our Saviour is born. Mountains in the Bible represent kingdoms, so the stone cut out without hands became a great kingdom and filled the whole earth. This fulfills the word given by Jesus to all His disciples: "And that repentance and remission of sins should be preached in His name among all nations, beginning at Jerusalem" (KJV Luke 24:47). With the birth of Jesus and the end of the four hundred silent years, we open the New Testament era in His - Story. Truly, as Jesus prophesied, the gospel of repentance has been preached to all nations. I pray this short version of His -Story of the four hundred silent years between the testaments helps in your understanding of God's Word and His wonderful plan of complete salvation for His creation man.

The book of Malachi was the last book of the Old Testament and the book ended with a curse. "Behold, I will send you Elijah the prophet before the coming of the great and dreadful day of the Lord: And he shall turn the heart of the fathers to the children, and the heart of the children to their fathers, lest I come and smite the earth with a curse" (KJV Malachi 4:5-6). These were God's last anointed words until the heavens opened and the angels spoke: "Glory to God in the highest, and on earth peace, good will toward men" (KJV Luke 2:14).

Some four hundred years passed between the curse that flowed from Malachi's pen and when the angels split the heavens singing glory to God in the highest. When we close the Old Testament and begin in Matthew nothing seems to be the same. The religious order of the day was the Pharisees, Sadducees, and Herodians of which no mention was made in the Old Testament. Rome was in power and the Jews were under a vicious king, Herod the Great, which was an Edomite, a descendant of Esau. Malachi, whose name means *"The messenger"*, was contemporary with Ezra and Nehemiah. By Malachi, Ezra and Nehemiah's writings we know the temple was restored and the ritual sacrifices had begun again.[45]

---

[45] Kirkpatrick, George. " Between The Testaments The Four Hundred Silent Years." *New Foundations Publication*. n. d. http://www.newfoundationspubl.org/between.htm (accessed June 11, 2013).

At times in life, there seems to be nothing going on and life seems to just be creeping along. When this happen is when we must become wide alert because as we know something is about to happen. In many instance, in the mist of calm, there comes all of a sudden this gigantic tidal wave of troubles. It is here *Wrestling In Deep Waters* is caused by the "[h]e that dasheth in pieces is come up before [our]face:[but we are to] keep the munition, watch the way, make thy loins strong, fortify thy power mightily" (KJV, Na 2:1). This again is why the scripture says as we know that there is always something always happening in deep of waters. The message given here to Ezekiel is not one of hopelessness. However, we cannot get to the other side of Jorden without the involved needing God's help. The *Wrestling in Deep Waters* was a major struggle under the law to/for the children of Israel. They needed need a savior. The stage throughout this 400 year period was about to climax. It is here where we are about to enter the dispensation of Grace; whereas, and, according to scripture:

"And he said unto me, Son of man, hast thou seen this? Then he brought me, and caused me to return to the brink of the river" (KJV, Ezekiel 47:6).

4th THOUSAND CUBITS

Man Under Grace

(See Luke 17:26-30; Luke 18:8; 2 Thess. 2:7-12; Rev. 3:15-16.) (See Jer. 30:5-7; Dan. 12:1; Zeph. 1:15-18; Matt. 24:21-22.)

"And he said unto me, Son of man, hast thou seen this? Then he brought me, and caused me to return to the brink of the river" (KJV, Ezekiel 47:6).

Ezekiel is at the "brink of the river," so are we, astill *"Wrestling In Deep Waters"* until the next with the "sufficiency of God's Grace."KJV, 2Cor 2:9). Not trying to be eloquent, "grace" is that which is just given to us; we did not deserve it; nor, can we earn it. "For by grace are ye saved through faith; and that not of yourselves: it is the gift of God: Not of works, lest any man should boast" (KJV Eph 2:8-9). This is "4th Thousand Cubits" of Ezekiel vision equaling the full mile that we all have and must travel before being crossed over to the other side of the river. This is life's reality, and This is heavy part of living! Ezekiel was in the water, and the water was above his head. To keep Ezekiel from drowning, God had Ezekiel (in the spirit or not) "back in a return to the brink of the river."

Ezekiel alone could not wrestle with these depths of waters because Ezekiel was still under the law, and these were not yet Ezekiel's waters. Did you get that?. To handle these waters one needs a lot of "grace."

As to these water deepening, *"for the waters had risen, waters to swim in, a river that could not be passed over"* (KJV, Ezekiel 47:5). Evangelically —as a paradox, there are many types of creatures in these waters and fish engorge. However, Ezekiel is only getting a sneak peak at all these things to be, but he wasn't ready for this wrestle that we wrestle with in our waters. Nevertheless, Ezekiel had his own wrestle, and he was already *"Wrestling in Deep Water."*

Let's jump into these waters and go for a swim, or, maybe, do a little fishing, as we wrestling with the turbulence of these deep waters in the boat. The living of life is a lifetime adventure. Grace is, in place, in the midst of these waters, to keep us—when we attempt to lose ourselves—detached to the principles of salvation. Most importantly Ezekiel can say is same as did Dr. King, "'For mine eyes have seen thy salvation,' Which thou hast prepared before the face of all people'" (KJV Lk 2:30-31).[46] The swimming is the entertaining moments of

---

[46] The New York Times: Dr. King. Martin Luther King Jr. January 15, 2013. http://topics.nytimes.com/topics/reference/timestopics/people/k/martin_luthe r_jr_king/index.html (accessed January 15, 2013).

the living under grace. The fishing is the working moments under grace. Wrestling with turbulence of these deep waters is sometimes right and sometimes wrong as grace keeps giving us another chance to get it right.

It is here where we must be careful because "grace" is not just a New Testament concept. The Lord from the very beginning extended his grace in the life of humanity. "But Noah found grace in the eyes of the LORD" (KJV Ge 6:8). It appears that grace is the final alternative to keep a person from eternal damnation. The road's end! Although in the time of Noah, humanity had options and could speak to God directly. This was at a time when these faith's waters had not risen to a depth of no crossing. Yet, in the first destroying act of God, "[G]OD saw that the wickedness of man was great in the earth, and that every imagination of the thoughts of his heart was only evil continually" (KJV Ge 6:5).

Despite the "evil continually" of man—and after the first destruction of man by God, God somehow came to the conclusion that "salvation for man" had to be tied to a savior and grace. Humanity was/is incapable of saving self. God had to act! Wright (2007) says, "[T]he Bible's description of God acting in salvation includes the whole of human life in every dimension and is not a mere life insurance policy for our souls after death" (p. 18).[47] A full study of the bible reveals that God had a plan to save us from ourselves. The information was given to Isaiah and states, "And it shall be said in that day, Lo, this is our God; we have waited for him, and he will save us: this is the LORD; we have waited for him, we will be glad and rejoice in his salvation" (KJV Isa 25:9).

Just as Ezekiel sees these waters rising, it is reasonable to say, "So did Isaiah!" Neither Ezekiel nor Isaiah had the depth of our present waters. Ezekiel on the brink of these waters look forward and across at waters too deep to stand up in and too wide to cross. I would guess that this made the wrestle that Ezekiel and Isaiah in the midst of was somewhat easy to go back and handle as a struggle. However, before the seeing of these present waters, their waters (Ezekiel and Isaiah), too, was a *"Wrestling in Deep Waters,"* but not as deep as these waters are today. The evil one has sown a great deal of "tares" among the "wheat." Not only are these waters deep, they are muddy too.

---

[47] Wright, Christopher J. H. *Salvation Belongs to Our God.* Edited by David Smith and John Scott. Downers Grove, Illinois: IVP Academic, 2007.

It is time for a cleansing of these waters, but for this to happen there has to be living water flowing in these waters from the giver of these life's waters. It does not get much deeper than this, does it? *"Afterward he measured a thousand; and it was a river that I could not pass over: for the waters had risen, waters to swim in, a river that could not be passed over"* (KJV, Ezekiel 47:5). A river that is full! It is here now, under/after the law, "Man Under Grace;" whereas, "[T]he fulness of the time was come, God sent forth his Son, made of a woman, made under the law, to redeem them that were under the law, that we might receive the adoption of sons" (KJV Gal 4:4-5). It is here we can shout, "Let the cleansing begin!" As the Son said to Paul, "[M]y grace is sufficient for thee. . ." (KJV 2 Co 12:9).

How polluted can a water become? Jesus gave us a parable to show us how polluted that these deep waters that we wrestle in, said:

So the servants of the householder came and said unto him, Sir, didst not thou sow good seed in thy field? From whence then hath it tares? He said unto them, An enemy hath done this. The servants said unto him, Wilt thou then that we go and gather them up? But he said, Nay; lest while ye gather up the tares, ye root up also the wheat with them. Let both grow together until the harvest: and at the time of harvest I will say to the reapers, Gather ye together first the tares, and bind them in bundles to burn them: but gather the wheat into my barn (KJV Mt 13:27-30).

Wrestling in Deep Waters is the mix pollution of "tares and wheat." *Wrestling in Deep Waters* is God's word watered down with the words of man. It is here as humanity is *Wrestling in Deep Waters*; grace is saying, "You did not earn me as you earn wages on some job!" Paul went on to drive this very point home by saying, "And if by grace, then is it no more of works: otherwise grace is no more grace. But if it be of works, then is it no more grace: otherwise work is no more work" (KJV Ro 11:6).

4th THOUSAND CUBITS

Now when I had returned, behold, at the bank of the river were very many trees on the one side and on the other. (KJV, Ezekiel 47:7).

Man Under the Personal Reign of Christ

(See Isa. 2:1-4; Isa. 11; Acts 15:14-17; Rev. 19:11-21; Rev. 20:1-6. (See Rev. 20:3,7-15; Rev. 21 and 22.).

This is near the time of shouting, and it is impossible not to give us vs. 8-9 with states:

(8)*Then said he unto me, These waters issue out toward the east country, and go down into the desert, and go into the sea: which being brought forth into the sea, the waters shall be healed.*

(9) *And it shall come to pass, that every thing that liveth, which moveth, whithersoever the rivers shall come, shall live: and there shall be a very great multitude of fish, because these waters shall come thither: for they shall be healed; and every thing shall live whither the river cometh.*

(10) *And it shall come to pass, that the fishers shall stand upon it from En-gedi even unto En-eglaim; they shall be a place to spread forth nets; their fish*

shall be according to their kinds, as the fish of the great sea, exceeding many (KJV Eze 47:8-10).

Here "Man Under the Reign of Christ" is the ministry of Jesus Christ with us still "*Wrestling in Deep Water*"—but in a personal relationship with Christ. This personal relationship begins with what the "Father" has brought together: "For God so loved the world that He gave His only begotten Son, that whoever believes in Him should not perish but have everlasting life" (John 3:16). The ministry of Jesus Christ is about living life as to our daily struggles toward the perfect—who rewards by giving us eternal life. Jesus preluded and asked the question: "And whosoever liveth and believeth in me shall never die. Believest thou this" (KJV Jn 11:26)? With the right answer, all things are possible henceforth and forever more. The reading of scripture that supports this acclamation says:

> And you, being dead in your trespasses and the uncircumcision of your flesh, He has made alive together with Him, having forgiven you all trespasses, having wiped out the handwriting of requirements that was against us, which was contrary to us. And He has taken it out of the way, having nailed it to the cross (Colossians 2:13-14). Therefore, If we live in the Spirit, let us also walk in the Spirit (KJV—Galatians 5:25).

We grow in grace moving toward perfection with the working cooperation of others within God, the Father. Jesus said, "Be ye therefore perfect, even as your Father which is in heaven is perfect" (KJV— Mt 5:48-6:1). This is the maturity that we all acquire in the working together with others and with God. This is the relationship with him that is personal, hands-on, and is fulfilled to the point of reward. Wheeler and Whaley (2011) stated, "Because God has placed [an] impulse in our heart, we can know Him and enjoy a relationship with Him that is personal and intentional."[48] Taking this a step further, it is the undoing, the incompleted, and the unsatisfied life that seek filling; even when, this life knows not what it needs until it is filled by faith. Nevertheless, life knows that it needs something. This something that life needs is only met at the introduction of Christ as one's personal savior. "Indeed I will make those of the synagogue of Satan, who say they are Jews and are not, but lie — indeed I will make them come and worship before your feet, and to know that I have loved you" (KJV— Rev. 3:9).

---

[48] David Wheeler and Vernon Whaley. *The Great Commission to Worship.* Nashville, Tennessee: B & H Publishing Group, 2011.

In the travel of time, it here that man evolves to the underage personal reign of Christ as the fisherman casting nets. It is we, as fish, are in need of being netted. Thes waters are deep, I tell you! These waters are above the ankle; these waters are above the knee; these waters are above the loins (waist); these waters are over the head; and these waters have become a river. This is the river of waters that traveled the spectrum of time, hewed out of eternity by God, for us, filled with tares planted among the wheat as we continue: *Wrestling In Deep Water*. Tares have polluted these waters finds Ezekiel standing in the midst thereof. These waters came down the corridors of time, twisted and turns, could be the Nile or maybe the **Jordon**. Let it be understood; unequivocally, God is in control, and we are saved by his grace that's through/in Jesus Christ.

This started off as a rocky journey for the children of God just prior to God's beginning as to speaking in parables to the children of God again. There had to be a birth. The first birth was the birth of John the Baptist. As we all know, John the Baptist was the cousin of Jesus Christ, and John the Baptist was also the forerunner of Jesus Christ. It is John the Baptist who baptized in this river of Jordan just before the swelling of the river. This river becomes a river that is too wide and deep to cross. This is the river that we wrestle with every day of our lives, metaphorically. The allegory and symbolism here is one of the old that fills the new with many viewpoints, cunnings, religions, and lie—to the point that it seems from time to time—are too unbearable. John the

Baptist saw "the Pharisees and Sadducees come to his baptism, and he said unto them, 'O generation of vipers, who hath warned you to flee from the wrath to come'" (KJV— Mt 3:7)?

The second birth is the birth of Jesus Christ. "For unto us a child is born, unto us a son is given: and the government shall be upon his shoulder: and his name shall be called Wonderful, Counselor, The mighty God, The everlasting Father, The Prince of Peace" (KJV— Isa 9:6). Then of years with us, man, under his reign, he speaks and says, "Thou sayest that I am a king. To this end was I born, and for this cause came I into the world, that I should bear witness unto the truth. Every one that is of the truth heareth my voice" (KJV—Jn 18:37). Isn't it interesting that Ezekiel is seeing all of this in the mist of this river. I don't know if "the man with the line in his hand"—with his faith— is standing on top of these waters as Jesus did in his ministry. Peter walked on water before looking at the wind. I do know what Ezekiel says, "And it shall come to pass, that every thing that liveth, which moveth, whithersoever the rivers shall come, shall live: and there shall be a very great multitude of fish, because these waters shall come thither: for they shall be healed; and every thing shall live whither the river cometh" (KJV —Ezekiel 47:9).

Living is the climax! As you read, you are alive; and, if, you are in Jesus Christ you are alive forevermore. Will your eternity be with God; or will, your eternity be below as a devil or demon with Satan has your Father? The choice is clear; there is no in between. Purgatory no longer exists. Purgatory was only for a short period of time and waited the resurrection of Jesus the Christ. Therefore, I say again, "living is the climax." Purgatory was state of rest in the upper region of Hades called "Sheol." "Like sheep they are appointed for Sheol; Death shall be their shepherd; straight to the grave they descend, and their form shall waste away; Sheol shall be their home" (KJV—Psa 49:14). In heaven we now go to the bosom of Jesus when we die, but prior to Jesus resurrection all that died went to Sheol and the bosom of Abraham.

There was a certain rich man, which was clothed in purple and fine linen, and fared sumptuously every day: And there was a certain beggar named Lazarus, which was laid at his gate, full of sores, And desiring to be fed with the crumbs which fell from the rich man's table: moreover the dogs came and licked his sores. And it came to pass, that the beggar died, and was carried by the angels into Abraham's bosom: the rich man also died, and was buried; And in hell he lift up his eyes, being in torments, and seeth Abraham afar off, and Lazarus in his bosom. And he cried and said, Father Abraham, have mercy on me, and send Lazarus, that he may dip the tip of his finger in water, and cool my tongue; for I am tormented in this flame. But Abraham said, Son, remember that thou in thy lifetime receivedst thy good things, and likewise Lazarus evil things: but now he is comforted, and thou art tormented. And beside all this, between us and you there is a great gulf fixed: so that they which would pass from hence to you cannot; neither can they pass to us, that would come from thence. Then he said, I pray thee therefore, father, that thou wouldest send him to my father's house: For I have five brethren; that he may testify unto them, lest they also come into this place of torment. Abraham saith unto him, They have Moses and the prophets; let them hear them. And he said, Nay, father Abraham: but if one went unto them from the dead, they will repent. And he said unto him, If they hear not Moses and the prophets, neither will they be persuaded, though one rose from the dead (KJV Lk 16:19-31).

In eternity and in living as to this climax means that we no longer go to the bosom of Abraham in hell (Sheol). This means that we now go the bosom of Jesus. I know we are wondering about those that died before Jesus' resurrection. Where are they now? Rest assured they too are with the Lord. Because while Jesus was in the grave before coming forth from the grave visited Hell to receive the captives setting them free. Scripture says:

When he [Jesus] ascended up on high, he led captivity captive, and gave gifts unto men. Now that he ascended, what is it but that he also descended first into the lower parts of the earth?

He that descended is the same also that ascended up far above all heavens, that he might fill all things (KJV Eph 4:8-10).

According to Buckley (2013) it is stated:

Despite Sheol's varying usages and contexts, there is a basic and the root meaning of the word. It's clear that the correct interpretation of the word is the name for a hell-like place or underworld. Sheol cannot be scripturally constructed to mean only a state of mind, or to represent an abstract concept such as death or chaos. Even though it is associated with the ground, it cannot be understood as simply a grave or literal pit. You would not dig a Sheol, because it is a realm of departed spirits.[49]

The Lord God is not a "Let-go-God" as is man or some want to be little [g]od. As Ezekiel wrestled in his own deep waters, the Lord said unto him:

What mean ye, that ye use this proverb concerning the land of Israel, saying, The fathers have eaten sour grapes, and the children's teeth are set on edge? As I live, saith the Lord GOD, ye shall not have occasion any more to use this proverb in Israel. Behold, all souls are mine; as the soul of the father, so also the soul of the son

---

[49] Buckley, Doug B. *Cupofwrath.com.* 2013. http://cupofwrath.com/risen-dust/01-hell-OT.php (accessed 7 17, 2013).

is mine: the soul that sinneth, it shall die (KJV Eze 18:2-4).

References

6000year.org. "Giants." 6000years.org: Amazing Bible
     Discoveries. n.d.
     http://www.6000years.org/frame.php?page=giants
     (accessed March 17, 2013).

Allstate. (2013). *Lincoln Benefit Life Company Info.* Retrieved
     February 16, 2013, from Allstate:
     https://www.accessallstate.com/anon/companyinfolbll.as
     px.

Baudrillard, Jean. "I: On Postmodernity." Modules on
     Baudrillard. n.d. Felluga, Dino. "Modules on Baudrillard:
     On Postmodernity." Introductory Guide to Critical
     Theory. Date of last update, which you can find on the
     home page. Purdue U. Date you accessed the site.
     <http://www.purdue.edu/guidetotheory/postmodernism/
     modules/ba (accessed April 4, 2013).

Biblos. *Bible Suite by Biblos: Westley Notes.* 2011.
     http://bible.cc/colossians/1-17.htm (accessed 1 25, 2013).

Biblestudytools. "Matthew Henry Commentary on the Bible:
     Ezekiel 47." *Bible Study Tools.* 2013.
     http://www.biblestudytools.com/commentaries/matthew-
     henry-complete/ezekiel/47.html (accessed February 17,
     2013).

BibleStudyTools. "Mathew Henry Commentary Ezekiel 47."
     Bible Study Tools.com: growing deep into the word.
     2013.
     http://www.biblestudytools.com/commentaries/matthew-

henry-complete/ezekiel/47.html (accessed February 15, 2013).

Biblestudytools. "Matthew Henry Commentary on the Bible: Ezekiel 47." *Bible Study Tools*. 2013. http://www.biblestudytools.com/commentaries/matthew-henry-complete/ezekiel/47.html (accessed February 22, 2013).

Boreal River. "WHITEWATER RESCUE TECHNICIAN (WRT) – 4 DAYS." *Boreal River*. 2013. http://borealriver.com/boreal-river-rescue-whitewater-swiftwater-training/technician-wrt-4days/ (accessed May 29, 2013).

Buckley, Doug B. *Cupofwrath.com*. 2013. http://cupofwrath.com/risen-dust/01-hell-OT.php (accessed 7 17, 2013).

Chabad-Lubavitch Media Center. "Yechezkel - Ezekiel - Chapter 1 verse 3." *The Jewish Complete Bible*. 2013. http://www.chabad.org/library/bible_cdo/aid/16099/jewish/Chapter-1.htm#v1 (accessed February 13, 2013).

Conjucture Corporation. "What is the Difference Between SMTP and POP?" *WiseGeek*. 2003-2013. http://www.wisegeek.com/what-is-the-difference-between-smtp-and-pop.htm (accessed April 21, 2013).

Dictionary.com. *Word Dictionary*. 2013. http://dictionary.reference.com/browse/religion (accessed January 8, 2013).

Dictionary.com. "pantheism." *Dictionary.com*. 2013.
http://dictionary.reference.com/browse/pantheism?s=t
(accessed February 2, 2013).

Dictionary.com. "God is Dead." Dictionary of Quotes. 2013.
http://quotes.dictionary.com/search/god_is_dead
(accessed March 9, 2013).

David Wheeler and Vernon Whaley. *The Great Commission to
Worship*. Nashville, Tennessee: B & H Publishing Group,
2011.

Embrace The Truth. "Theology > Sin > Reality of Satan > Fall
from Heaven." Embraced by Truth...Reflections on
Theology and Life. n. d.
http://www.embracedbytruth.com/Sin/Reality%20of%2
0Satan/Fall%20from%20Heaven.htm (accessed March
18, 2013).

Encyclopedia Britannica, Inc. *Encyclopedia Britannica*. Chicago:
London: Toronto: William Benton, 1960.

Farlex. *Threshold: The Free Dictionary by Farlex*. 2013.
http://www.thefreedictionary.com/threshold (accessed
February 22, 2013).

Friedrich Nietzsche "The Origins of Herd Morality" in P Singer
(ed). *Ethics*. Oxford University Press. NY 1994

George F. Koob, Ph.D. *What Is Pleasure?* October 13, 2010.
http://www.dana.org/news/cerebrum/detail.aspx?id=291
96 (accessed August 7, 2013).

Huxman, Karlyn Kohrs Campbell and Susan Schultz. *The
Rhetorical Act: Thinking, Speaking, and Writing*

Critically. Belmont,CA: Wadsworth Cengage Learning, 2009.

Hammer, Frank L. *Life and Its Mysteries*. Forgotten Books, 1945.

Herder, Johann Gottfried. *Outlines of a Philosophy of the History of Man*. New York: Bergman Publishers, 1800.

inrebus.com. *Latin quotes, mottos and words of wisdom*. 2007. http://www.inrebus.com/latinphrases_a.php (accessed January 8, 2013).

Kandel, R. S. (2003). Water From Heaven. Chichester, New York, U.S.A.: Columbia United Press.

Kirkpatrick, George. " Between The Testaments The Four Hundred Silent Years." *New Foundations Publication*. n. d. http://www.newfoundationspubl.org/between.htm (accessed June 11, 2013).

LaRocco, Chris, and Blair Rothstein. *The Big Bang*. n. d. http://www.umich.edu/~gs265/bigbang.htm (accessed January 27, 2013).

Leadershipwithyou. "Martin Luther King Junior Leadership Case Study." Leadership With You. 2008–2013. http://www.leadership-with-you.com/martin-luther-king-junior-leadership.html (accessed March 29, 2013).

Marrs, Texe. *America Being Torn Down and Rebuilt*. 2012.
    http://www.texemarrs.com/022010/rothschilds_plan.htm
    (accessed January 8, 2013).

Matthew Henry's Commentary on the Whole Bible: New
    Modern Edition, Electronic Database. Copyright (c) 1991
    by Hendrickson Publishers, Inc.).

McCarthy, Michael & Carter, Ronald. ""There's millions of
    them": hyperbole in everyday conversation."
    ScienceDirect. 2003.

http://www.sciencedirect.com/science/article/pii/S037821660300
    1164 (accessed Jan McCarthy, Michael & Carter, Ronald.
    ""There's millions of them": hyperbole in everyday
    conversation." *ScienceDirect*. 2003.
    http://www.sciencedirect.com/science/article/pii/S037821
    6603001164 (accessed January 13, 2013). Febuary 13,
    2013).

Morton, Timothy S. "Chapter I: Legalism Verses Liberty." From
    Liberty to Legalism. 1999.
    http://www.biblebelievers.com/Morton_legalism-
    liberty.html (accessed March 8, 2013).

NOAA. "Oceans." NOAA: National Ocean and Atmospheric
    Administration. n. d. http://www.noaa.gov/ocean.html
    (accessed March 12, 2013).

Paul Przyborski & Warren Wiscombe. "A Multi-Phased
    Journey." *Nasa Earth Observatory*. 2009.

http://earthobservatory.nasa.gov/Features/Water/page2.
php (accessed February 18, 2013).

PhD., Howard Thurman. The Inward Journey. 9 vols.
Richmond, IN: Friends United Press, 1971.

Robinson, B. A. *Some theories on the origin of religion.* March 15,
2009. http://www.religioustolerance.org/rel_theory1.htm
(accessed January 10, 2013).

Scofield, C I. "The Seven Dispensations." *Biblecentre.org* .
October 28, 2006.
Http://www.biblecentre.org/topics/cis_rd_2_seven_disp.h
tm (accessed April 4, 2013).

Shreeve, Jamie. "Ardi Surrounded by Family." *National
Geographic News.* October 28, 2010.

http://news.nationalgeographic.com/news/2009/10/091001-
oldest-human-skeleton-ardi-missing-link-chimps-
ardipithecus-ramidus.html (accessed April 3, 2013).

Simmons, Lorna. "Ancient Time Keepers." University Lowbrow
Astronomers. June 2009.
http://www.umich.edu/~lowbrows/reflections/1999/lsimmons.2.h
tml (accessed March 17, 2013).

Smith, David John. "How Does God Speak to Us? 33 Ways
from Faith That Takes." *shelboese.org.* 2011.

http://shelboese.org/how-does-god-speak-to-us-33-ways/
(accessed June 3, 2013).

Stardate. "Meteorites." *StarDate*. n.d. http://stardate.org/astro-guide/ssguide/meteorites (accessed March 2, 2013).

Stephanie Sarkis, Ph.D. "50 Quotes on Consequences." Psychology Today. April 22, 2012. ww.psychologytoday.com/blog/here-there-and-everywhere/201204/50-quotes-consequences (accessed March 16, 2013).

Stevens, Mitchell. *Without Gods: toward a history of disbelief*. October 18, 2006. http://www.futureofthebook.org/mitchellstephens/archives/2006/10/pleasure_v_reli.html (accessed January 9, 2013).

The New York Times: Dr. King. *Martin Luther King Jr.* January 15, 2013. http://topics.nytimes.com/topics/reference/timestopics/people/k/martin_luther_jr_king/index.html (accessed January 15, 2013).

Wright, Christopher J. H. *Salvation Belongs to Our God*. Edited by David Smith and John Scott. Downers Grove, Illinois: IVP Academic, 2007.

About the Author

Sherman A. Jones (Author) is currently working on his **Masters Degree** in Higher Education: Teaching on the Collegiate Level. Mr. Jones is currently president of Cbookspublishing and Bookstore.

The author, Sherman A. Jones has the following degrees:
- ➢ B. S. —Paralegal Studies
- ➢ B. S. —Theology
- ➢ A. S. —Radio and Television Broadcasting
- ➢ A. S. —Electronic Technology

The author, Sherman A. Jones, holds a lifetime FCC license.

www.ingramcontent.com/pod-product-compliance
Lightning Source LLC
Chambersburg PA
CBHW021222090426
42740CB00006B/342